Full Tilt Living

Full Tilt Living

Live in the moment,
even when it STINKS!
Find the juicy parts and
let the world know YOU ARE HERE.

Maureen Smith

Red Wheel
Boston, MA / York Beach, ME

First published in 2001 by Red Wheel/Weiser, LLC
P. O. Box 612
York Beach, ME 03910-0612
www.redwheelweiser.com

Library of Congress Cataloging-in-Publication Data

Smith, Maureen (Maureen J.).
    Full tilt living / Maureen Smith.
        p. cm.
    ISBN 1-59003-000-1 (pbk. : alk.paper)
    1. Conduct of life. I. Title.

BF637.C5 S545 2001
158.1--dc21   2001031834

Typeset in Adobe Garamond
Cover and text design by Jill Feron/Feron Design
Cover art: Top: copyright © SuperStock
Bottom: copyright © EyeWire, Inc.
Illustrations: copyright © EyeWire, Inc.

Printed in the United States of America

MV

08 07 06 05 04 03 02 01
 8 7 6 5 4 3 2 1

The paper used in this publication meets the minimum requirements of
the American National Standard for Information Sciences-Permanence of
Paper for Printed Library Materials Z39.48-1992 (R1997).

Dedication

To Sydney, the woman with wings,
and Frank, the wildest child on Chestnut Street.

Acknowledgments

This book would never have happened without the imagination of my publisher, Jan Johnson, and the support of my daughter, Sydney, who gave Jan my newsletters. I also want to thank Sydney for having so much faith in her mom that she set up a Web-site for me. And one more thank you to Jan for finding a way to squeeze four more chapters out of me and then enduring my embarrassingly prima donna-like behavior during the editing.

Contents

Introduction

from where I stand, experiencing life as full and rich is a moment-to-moment kind of thing. That means getting the most out of day-to-day, business-as-usual living. Being as centered and healthy and fully alive on all levels for as long as possible every day.

The ideas I offer in *Full Tilt Living* are based on what I have learned along the way. Some of them come from my own personal road testing. Some from issues I have helped clients wind their way through. Many of them started as a newsletter I wrote for my clients as a vehicle to give them encouragement and fresh insights.

The first chapters address the day-to-day things we all encounter. These run the gamut from getting

Get past the speed bumps without biting your tongue.

up and going in the morning to guidance on managing more hair-raising "Mother said there'd be days like this" stuff. Then what follows are some invitations to explore and expand the way you are in the world. The last chapters present doorways to what I might call finding your bliss: meditation and connecting with sources of strength outside the everyday world.

I suggest you work your way through the chapters a few pages at a time, in the order they're written. If some idea appeals, try it, play with it for a while before you go on. If it doesn't appeal, feel free to skip it.

I am hoping that you will find chapters here that will help get you past the speed bumps and other such diversions that might break your stride and take you away from finding the delight in your life. It is my wish that these pages will give you the opportunity to discover ways to find a richness that you did not know could be yours. Full tilt living! Ours to enjoy!

chapter 1
Tapping Your Power Source

What kind of steam do you use to drive your engine? I mean, how do you go about getting up and running every day?

Unless you are a Disney character, you've probably felt that "I can't do another day of this" sensation. It usually hits me right after the alarm clock beeps (they used to ring, but this is a new age, believe me).

I admit that it isn't every day I encounter that urge to spend the day with the bedbugs. A day when my whole plan is spending big chunks of money on things that have absolutely *nothing* to do with dentists or auto mechanics, or getting to roll out to the redwoods for a full day of air and trees and ham sandwiches with root beer (anybody

Instead of seeding your fear clouds, take a walk in the sunshine.

who comes along usually brings their own food in self-defense) gets me past that first blast of "what am I doing here?!!" consciousness pretty quickly.

But let's say it's a day when under the covers looks like the best place to be. What then? It could be that you let a fat, threatening cloud of fear hang over you. It is pretty easy to let that fear cloud with all of the "what ifs" you have so skill-fully seeded it with rain right down on you: "I have to get up now and get to work in that rattle trap of a car. I just know the grinding noise it's been making is going to cost me a bundle to fix. What if it takes all the money I'm saving for my vacation?" Or "What if I do such a horrible job at work today that I get fired? I'll have to move to a dumpy little hovel on a dirt road and live on beans and whatever I can grow in the garden—that is if I can get anything worth eating to grow—and wear clothes from the thrift store and live without cable." This is a little over the top, I realize. But I wouldn't be surprised if you have your own ver-sion of the "Fear Engine."

No one can terrify you quite as well as *you* can. And after one of those little sessions with yourself, you have so much adrenaline pumping through your system, the only thing you can do is rocket out of bed. You head off to work steaming like a demon. You have shot past "I think I can, I think I can!" and straight to "*This train's a-comin'*!"

Make no mistake, though. Being fueled by fear causes some heavy emotional wear and tear. And it may not keep you going past lunchtime. So another terror session over lunch, right? If you use the Fear Engine often enough, you can completely destroy your natural, healthy work-rest rhythm. And you will very likely lose the sense of joy and accomplishment in what you do along with that natural rhythm. Life might, as I have heard it said, begin to seriously suck.

Wouldn't it be great to tune into a different frequency altogether? How about replacing the fear with a more natural fuel? Give the Power Check List a try. And you can stay right there in bed to do it if you want.

The basic idea behind the Power Check List is to connect as completely as possible with your immensely valuable gifts and strengths—so what gives you a jump start on the day and fuels you right on through to the end comes from your deepest, truest source—not from skimming off the adrenaline you manufacture for yourself from a good scare.

In some ways, your Power Check List is similar to what you hope the mechanics are doing before your plane takes off. It's best if you write your own for exactly the same reasons that your personalized Fear Engine works so well: Nobody knows what counts the most for you as well as you do yourself. But I've created a little outline to help you get started.

THE POWER CHECK LIST PROCESS
Step 1: Tuning into Your Physical Power Plant
Begin with the breathing part of you and fill your lungs with a slow, luxurious, deep breath. Now hold it for a couple of heartbeats and then as you slowly let the breath out, check into how basically good it felt to fill yourself up with oxygen. Repeat this until you can notice the heaviness leaving your body.

At this point I usually find myself wanting a good stretch. So do that, taking time to admire how responsive your muscles are. Spread your arms out as far as you can, make fists, and tighten all the muscles from your fingers to your shoulder blades. Now that you've done horizontal, do vertical. Squeeze toes, feet, calves, thighs, buns, abs. Then pull your shoulders down away from your ears as far as you can. Of course, you are getting some good breathing in here too.

Feeling awake? Great! Do not be tempted to let your mind jump in here and tear off in other directions. Stay with your waking-up body. At this point I like to play with seeing if I can "hear" it humming, like the well-tuned engine in an Indy racecar. If you're alone, or if you don't mind looking a little silly to whoever might be with you, go ahead and make some car sounds. Or if you see yourself as more the locomotive type, try some train whistles.

Step 2: Count Your Inner Blessings

Now while that motor of yours is humming, count your inner blessings. These are not the same as the outer ones that everyone tells you to count when they want you to cheer up. Those aren't the blessings that matter. You are going to let the wonderful stuff that you admire about yourself bubble up—your fine way of conquering computer glitches, your pinpoint accuracy with figures, your uncanny ability to be at the right place at the right time, your fabulous sense of humor.

These may change from day to day. And really, I find fresher is better. It lets me keep pace with what might be going on for me on that day so that I can reference my inner blessings checklist if I hit a rough spot later on. For example, if I pointed out to myself just that morning that I can be incredibly calm even when I'm completely lost, it makes

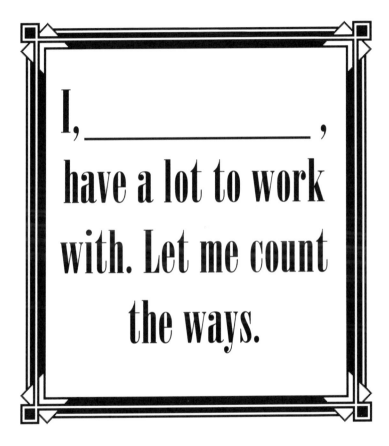

I, _____ ,
have a lot to work
with. Let me count
the ways.

it much easier to deal with the confusion that happens when I lose my sense of direction.

I have to say that this is no guarantee that the people with you will admire your ability to stay calm in such a situation if you are the driver and they are the drivees. Misreading two exit signs in a row, thus causing you to wind up in the wrong city, can really put a strain on people. Everything has its limits . . . but I digress. What are your inner blessings today?

Once you have a healthy list of things that you admire, do it. Admire yourself. Say, "Wow! I've got some great stuff to work with here!"

Step 3: Find Your Core

Find your core and notice its strength. Some imagination is useful here. You might experience your core as an energy located in the center of your body, or as an energy "rod" running from the top of your head down to the soles of your feet. It may have a sensation of warmth for you, or it may have a color that it radiates, or a note that it sounds.

Once you have a sense of your core, let it travel out until it makes a sort of energy field or envelope around you. You might notice it as beams of light radiating. It might seem similar to electricity. It might have a sensation of a spreading warmth. You might even notice sounds. The size of the envelope can change from day to day.

Check it out and see if you can find its outer edge. Stay with this for a few minutes if you can. You may find that you can call it up during the day if you need to recharge, or you might not notice it at all as things get busy.

Step 4: Connect with the Positive (optional)

If it suits you, you may want to finish up your power check by spending a moment tuning into what you draw strength from in the world around you. I'm very conscious of my environment—so I like to tap into the power of the "atmosphere" around me, sort of drawing energy up through the soles of my feet and all the way up through my core, then letting it make a fountain out of the top of my head. It sounds a little silly, like I've turned myself into a giant sprinkler, but it is kind of fun. Your final check may involve connecting with the universe or people who are important to you, or being prayerful.

By now you may be thinking, "Sure, this Power Check List sounds great, but it's going to take a lot of time I don't have!" It actually can be done in very few minutes.

Here's an outline you can use if you like that kind of thing:

1. Tune into your physical power plant with full, slow breaths; stretches; and appropriate vocalizations.

2. Review your checklist of your abilities and what you admire about them.

3. Tap into your core energy and allow it to radiate out.

4. Connect with the positive elements/relationships in your universe.

How often does it make sense to do this? I leave that one up to you. More is probably better. If you decide to use the Power Check List on a daily basis, remember to keep it fresh for yourself.

Vary your stretches. Gathering into a ball and then letting everything fly out at the same time is a good one. Some sideways rolls might be fun to try too.

The abilities or inner blessings you choose to note can be targeted at the day's projects, of course. You will probably find that the experience of your core energy and the way it radiates out changes on its own. And connections with positive elements will probably adjust themselves as well.

Mostly, this is a time to be playful and spend a few moments with the best parts of yourself before your focus goes to the million things that make up your day.

chapter 2
Living in the
Spaces In-Between

It seems that the really juicy parts of living happen not in the big chunks of time that we all spend taking care of the business we must do to earn a living and keep ourselves and our living spaces and those we take care of whole and happy— but in the smaller time segments in-between.

Like the night this summer that I looked up at the sky just before I pulled into my driveway and saw the hugest, most spectacular moon I have ever seen hanging over the city and making the skyline look like a picture postcard. It did take a few heart-beats to soak it all in. I was a changed woman by the time I parked my car.

What I am saying here, without getting any more dramatic, is that those few seconds with the moon in my eyes (like a big pizza pie, yes) were so rich and so revitalizing and so very unexpected. And very likely the best part of that day. So why not have moments like that more often? The opportunities for them are all around. I can tell you that if I'm playing reruns in my head, I miss out on a lot. What I mean is that if we're rehashing stuff that happened recently or re-worrying about the things we always worry about, with our needles stuck in one of their familiar grooves, we're not there for those tiny spectacular happenings. We have to be ready for them, and at times we have to make them happen.

Like yesterday, when I was standing in a long cafeteria line with a huge number of other shoppers longing for a bowl of hot soup and a place to (YES!) *sit down*.

I took myself up on an uninspired thought to count the number of people between me and my lunch, and when I got to the folks just in front of me, my thoughts and my energy level were skidding into an all-time low.

But wait! There in front of me, all snuggled into his baby carrier, was a hairless little lump of baby with scrunched-up fists and eyes that said he was about to go critical in his mother's arms. I got down low and looked in his eyes and gave him my best smile and coo. I could tell he was checking out this new thing. (I was hoping he was reading me as "friendly woman" and not "creature crouching for attack.") His mouth went slack for a moment, and then he let loose with one beautiful toothless baby grin. I lost count of my place in line and shared an "Isn't he just wonderful?" smile and nod with his mom, and the world didn't seem nearly as prickly a place.

What's in your spaces in between?

What do you say to giving this living in the spaces in-between a run?

The big chunks of your life—getting a work project done, losing twenty pounds, quitting smoking, taking care of a houseful of people—are going to go smoother if you take a few moments to dive into those in-between spaces.

I warn you in advance that if you let on to what you're doing, people might suspect you of being on some kind of drug trip, ("WOW!!! Do you *believe* how great this flower smells?? I mean it's *unreal!!!*" could give people the wrong impression.) so I suggest keeping it to yourself. They'll get the benefit of the aftereffects without you saying anything.

SEVEN-DAY PLAN

How do you find time to make those spaces in-between happen? Plan, of course! No, I'm not talking about a spa weekend. I don't know about you, but the work it would take for me to pull that off would probably put me into so much stress overload that I'd be lucky to break even on the stress scale by the end of it. Take out your weekly planner (of course you have one—they're great stress reducers) and treat yourself to a special "in-between event" every day. Plan the event and the time and write it in, just like any other important activity you might have on your schedule.

Here, I'll do the first week for you:

Day 1: Give yourself three uninterrupted minutes to enjoy looking at snapshots of people who bring joy to your life. (Notation in planner: Snapshots)

Day 2: Do the Mona Lisa: Sit in a comfortable position, close your eyes, and briefly turn up the corners of your mouth like Mona Lisa. All the muscles in your face will relax, and that's where you carry the most tension. (Notation in planner: Mona Lisa)

Day 3: Do that old-fashioned thing that gentlefolk used to do: "Take in the air." Simply put, go for a walk and breathe deeply, getting good and oxygen-rich. You'll feel renewed! (Notation in planner: Take in the Air)

Day 4: Make yourself a hot cup of tea and do nothing but drink it. No distractions, just you and a fragrant, hot cup of tea. (Notation in planner: Tea)

Day 5: Read jokes for three minutes. Laugh out loud. It could be the funnies. Better yet, get a joke book and keep it close by. Laughter is healing, you know. (Notation in planner: Jokes)

Day 6: Buy yourself a flower. Go for a color you find irresistible and also your favorite fragrance if you can tolerate scents. Put it in a vase close by you so you can touch it and inhale its perfume all day. (Notation in planner: Flower)

Day 7: Give your hands a massage, both the backs of your hands and your palms.

Then massage each finger, starting at the base and working out to the fingertip. This is even more wonderful when you use lotion! (Notation in planner: Hand Massage)

I'm sure by now you're getting the hang of this and can create a Seven-Day Plan that is tailored to your taste. Try it for a week. If you like it, make it part of your weekly schedule.

MAGICAL PLACES

If you find that the pace of your life becomes overwhelmingly challenging and there is no such thing as "in-between," lay out some locations in your landscape that let you shift out of overdrive. Make some magical places, little islands to be delighted in, where you can recharge. Places of light for yourself. Let them be just yours. Let them be simple. Take pages from your cat's book and spread them through your daily "territory." And if you have never lived with a cat (there is no such thing as owning one, you know), ask someone who has how it works, this seeding of your territory.

Their doorways can be objects that lead you to places where you can mentally hunker down into for a few safe, unobserved seconds of respite. They can be treasures in the giant size or treasures that look to the naked eye more like trash.

Or they can be memories. Make the memories sweet ones, with maybe some nostalgia mixed in. One of my favorites is a memory as a four-year-old visiting San Juan Capistrano Mission with my grandmother, who was never without a dark blue, velvet hat pinned firmly to her head when she was outdoors. I actually have a snapshot of her wearing it as she lounged with us (in a dress and black grandma shoes) on a blanket at the beach. So we were in the Mission garden, she and I, when she sat me down on a bench. I looked up just as a flock of predatory pigeons came in for their usual dive at the tourists. There were wings everywhere, and in the middle of them all was Grammy with a very fat pigeon plopped right in the middle of that blue velvet hat. What I remember best is how she laughed and laughed. It's an in-between moment I can go back to time and again.

Treasures large could be favorite breathtaking views in photos, or wearing jewelry that you would not otherwise show up at work in. Treasures small might be a rock you love, an origami bird made with newspaper, your favorite marble. Touch them, let them be your focus and lift you into the magic they hold for you, just long enough to let that magic soak in and fill you up. So you go from prunish to plump, like a raisin magically turning back into a grape. Well, you get the idea, I'm sure.

TIPS FOR FINDING MORE IN-BETWEEN SPACES

Now that you have the idea, here are a few more ways that you can discover in-between moments:

Getting Warm Inside When It's Cold Out

Set up a special place for yourself to acknowledge how you enjoy the relationships you have with the special people in your life. You can make it virtual, as in a space you visualize and go to in an imaginative way to "tap into" the richness of those relationships, or you might want to make it actual. A table with pictures or momentos, a wall of photos for remembered moments.

Let more warmth in by snatching a few moments to enjoy the warmth of a good friend's voice on the phone, with feeling the flood of warmth in your favorite music, with the unmatchable warmth of sharing laughter, with touching in on your own heart, vision, personal passion.

Making Your Way through
the Holiday Party Muck

This is one for the big holiday party season. It must be that lots of folks like lots of parties, because there are so many between December and January. I have noticed a pretty high level of grumbling about having to go to yet another party, however, so you party lovers may be in the minority. If you belong to the grumbling segment of the population, let me suggest that you take it a little easy on yourself. You have lots of company, you know. So when you get to the party that you dragged yourself to, look for the person in the crowd that looks like they're enjoying it about as much as you are and spend a little time lightening their load. Tell them something sincerely nice you noticed about them. Share a funny anecdote if you have one. Look pleased to meet them if you don't. Then move on and do it with someone else. It should make the event more fun for you. It could possibly cause you to shift from well-tuned party grumbler to that oh-so-coveted category, Life of the Party. Watch out, lampshades!!!

Relate to Air

Blow bubbles. Every now and again, sneak a chunk of bubble gum and blow yourself an occasional bubble when the coast is clear. It's hard to say whether it's the pleasure of being bad or the exquisite moment of forming that filmy, soft mini-cushion that does it. Or get a jar of bubble soap and blow a long string of them. Blow them in the air and watch them float and dance. Blow them on friends. Hope they laugh. Let them blow some too.

Just Feel Good

Spend a day thanking people and telling them why you appreciate what they did. Or skip the thank-you and just tell people what you appreciate. Do this for your own benefit—it will make you feel pretty great. It will also point out to you that: (*a*) people do caring things for you, and (*b*) you often miss the caring things people do. You can enjoy those caring acts much more if you see them. It may lead to some of your own.

chapter 3
Slicing through the Fog

You got a problem? Can you imagine a day in your life without one? We manage hundreds with hardly a wrinkle in our forehead. We are in control and loving it! Isn't that what success is all about? Isn't this how our lives should be?

Yes, it is. I believe that's why a problem we can't see our way through can throw us off balance and make us feel so powerless. Confusion may be a higher state, but it sure is a bumpy ride.

So what can you do when your usually crystal-clear vision suddenly becomes a tulle fog so dense you can't see your hand in front of you? It's a real challenge to know what your next move should be when you're trying to work through that emotional haze you encounter when you can't see a

MOANING, SIGHING, weeping, tearing at your hair and clothing are SADLY underrated these days.

good solution on the horizon. That particular challenge can loom large and seem especially threatening to your well-being. It can produce a nasty twisted feeling in your stomach and cause you to jerk awake in the middle of the night. It can make you edgy and short-tempered. Definitely not yourself. And you want your breezy I-love-life-and-everyone-in-it self back! What can you do? Here are some ideas:

➤ **Talk it out.** You are not alone. (Isn't that a song by a well-known artist?) Find someone who will listen and talk about it. If the listener you have chosen isn't acquainted with how powerful listening in a compassionate, non-problem-solving way can be, you'll have to educate him or her. Be clear that you need someone to bounce some ideas off of. Just to listen to you, not give advice. Then let 'er rip.

You might have to gently remind your listener once or twice that you just need a chance to vent if this is a new experience for them. It often happens that you begin to see some solutions by the end of the session. You will definitely feel lighter. And that's good, right?

➤ **Give yourself room to feel absolutely horrible.** Do a fine job of it. Moaning, sighing, weeping, tearing at your hair and clothing are sadly underrated these days. Part of what is creating the "fog" for you is an emotional overload that you have created by imagining that your problem is either not solvable or will be much too painful for you to deal with. You need to dump some of that stress that is paralyzing your problem-solving skills. So try outdoing Elmer Fudd and his "Woe is me!" Promise yourself as you start that you will get down to business as soon as you're finished gnashing your teeth.

➤ **Do some visualizations.** Energy work pays big dividends when you're problem solving. This works best when you can be as far removed from "ordinary reality" as possible. Choose a time and place where you can be quiet and uninterrupted for a half hour or so.

1. First get very calm (the opposite of your ranting and raving self). Put on some soothing music; turn down the lights; and do some slow, deep breathing. If you like to use candles, get them out. A little incense might not hurt, either. Use them to help you set a mood just for you.

2. Now allow the issue that is before you to appear as energy. Take a little time with

this. Try to suspend your judgment of how things should look. People have seen big, oozy blobs; a jumble of twisted, wiry lines; a dense gray fog; monsters. You name it.

3. When an image has formed, choose a color of light and wrap it all around it. Simply put light around it and hold it, completely contained in that strong, clear light for a few moments.

4. Now let the whole thing go.

5. Once your visualization has faded and while you are in such a wonderful, nurturing frame of mind, take a few moments to acknowledge your inner strength, the wisdom you have gained, the skills you have achieved. Enjoy who you are! End your session with a tension-relieving stretch. Repeat this process as often as it seems right to you.

➤ **Chart it.** Write your problem down as a heading on a sheet of paper and underneath, write the date you want to have the final solution. Then list solutions as they come to you. You might have some right away, or they may dribble in over days. Don't reject any of them. Make yourself a nice long list. If one of them lights up as you are reading

Take a deep breath and make the

BEST

choice you can!

them over, voilà! Problem solved! If it's a particularly gnarly problem, circle the solutions you like the most and take them to someone whose judgment you trust on the date you have assigned. Discuss the pros and cons of each. Then take a deep breath and make the best choice you can. Sometimes doing the best you can at the moment moves the problem forward and gives you an opportunity to approach it again with more resources or insights than you had on the first go-around.

Oh, and remember that old standby, imagining your problem as the heading on the front page of the newspaper. Doing this can sometimes knock it down to a manageable size for you: "Neighborhood Mutt Impregnates Champion Rotweiler," "IRS Writes Threatening Letter," "Front Teeth Must Be Replaced," "Employee Files Lawsuit," "Entire Family Drops in for Surprise Visit While Flea Infestation Reaches New Heights . . ."

Here's the condensed version:

- Get someone to listen. No advice, just listen in a compassionate, nonjudgmental way.

- Weep and wail and gnash your teeth. Feel completely, overwhelmingly, noisily sorry for yourself.

- Visualize!

- Chart out potential solutions.

- Acknowledge that problems sometimes can only be tackled in steps. Honor yourself for making the best decision you can at the time. Recognize that sometimes issues need time to evolve. And so may you.

chapter 4
How to Succeed at Failure

What do you do when things don't work out the way you wanted them to? Or more to the point: What do you do when you fail? Ouch!!! I like version number one much better— "Not my fault; I made my best effort; there were factors beyond my control."

Just for the sake of argument, let's say that hiding behind door number one in a private part of your outlook on things there lies an element of the "F" word. You have failed!!! You should have, you could have, you didn't, you wish you had! Dark, heavy thoughts. And not really very helpful, unless you are hoping for an ulcer.

Not that failure doesn't have its good points. For some perverse reason, humans remember lessons learned in failure much more fully than we do lessons learned in success. If we can get past the pain and see their forest through our trees, that is. Like if you put your hand on a hot stove, you may not necessarily give up cooking. You may pay more attention to the controls or have a more healthy respect for the meaning of "high," but you will probably keep right on frying and boiling.

So, back to the question, what do we do when we fail? I'm guessing you have developed ways to get some good out of your goofs. Here are some of my favorites:

➤ Go ahead and admit to yourself that you flopped, missed the mark, blew it, made mush out of macaroni. It will take the sting out and give you the advantage of being ready to get the good stuff out of the experience. Your trees will be starting to look more like a forest right away!

➤ Give yourself a little mental nudge by telling yourself "This is great!" but don't be sarcastic about it. Really mean it. Your subconscious mind will shift gears from crouching for the blow to looking for the important information you can get from having a failure (e.g., burners produce lots of cooking heat at a moment's notice).

➤ You may need to switch Big and Little for yourself before you go any further. You want to be the "Big." Failure has a way of making humans feel they are shrinking. Jack the Giant Killer may not have had a problem with this, but the rest of us do. So let yourself grow back to a more normal size. Take a look at the area where there has been a failure. If it seems to be looming large, shrink it to "Little." If you didn't find yourself shrinking as you looked at things and the failure appears not to be unnervingly large, feel free to skip this part.

➤ Time for the interview! It's good to take notes when you do this so you don't miss any useful information. Choose questions that can give you specifics. Start with "Why is this great?" and see if a list doesn't develop. Try other versions, like "What have I gained from this?" Move on to "How would I do this next time?" And don't forget the interview question that I admit makes me want to hurl but produces great results: "Is there anything

Fail big!
   Fail often!
You'll learn
      wonderful
         things!

else?" When you've exhausted that one, you're done.

➤ Let it go. Congratulate yourself for taking the risks that allowed for the possibility of failure or success in the first place. Reap the rewards from the lessons you have learned. Take that wheat and let go of that chaff! Be fully in the next moment of your life, not in the moments—no matter how earthshaking—you have just lived. You'll sleep well if you do this. And will know things that you could not have learned as well any other way. This, by the way, is something that is a basic part of the lives of successful people.

Now I'm feeling a little like a coach on a football team. So go out there and go for it! Fail big! Fail often! You'll learn wonderful things!

chapter 5

Keeping Your Engine Purring

f you were a car, it would be pretty easy to lay out what you need to run well: tune-ups for your engine and regular oil changes, right? The good news here is that you are not confined in a box of steel, smelling of oil and drinking unleaded by the gallon. You are a much sleeker, more versatile machine. You can change your shape, eat virtually anything you like to keep your engine running, and drop by a perfume counter for a fragrance change. The bad news is that it's all in your hands to come up with your best formula to be in peak condition. This has led to the spawning (okay, birth) of health clubs, diet centers, publications, TV programs, star videos, and lots of amazing sports fashions. Have we hit information overload? Let's be simple about this.

1. **Drink water like a fish.**
2. **Eat your vegetables.**
3. **Exercise regularly.**
4. **Sleep well.**

1. DRINK

First of all let me say that I *know* fish don't drink water, but don't let that stop you. I used to think that I was a hopelessly crabby person because I would feel so low when I got out of bed in the morning. Then I started drinking a glass of water as soon as I got up and discovered that even *I* could be more or less perky first thing in the morning. I have to say that I was sort of attached to my little image of myself as a deep, demented person and was surprised and feeling pretty sheepish when I found out what one glass of water could do.

With water, more is better. Drink the eight glasses someone came up with as the magic number and see how it goes. In the back of my mind, I've always wondered if it's the water that you drink with the aspirin or the aspirin itself that helps a headache . . .

2. EAT

Vegetables. You can eat fruit if you don't like them. Really, you have lots to choose from here. I have noticed that experts on nutrition seem to pick favorite foods and go on at incredible lengths about how powerful, necessary, and vitamin-packed their particular choices are. Some of them seem to be more in the vegetable camp. Some of them root more for fruits. I do respect what they have come up with to keep me healthy. But the truth is, if it doesn't taste good to me, I still won't eat it. So I go for variety and choose a fruit when the vegetable doesn't sing for me. Go ahead and choose what you like. And have some every day.

Now if you are a purist about getting some F&V from each of the possible categories, but you, like I, don't love them all, you can always smother vegetables in butter or sauce and get them down that way. Your cholesterol level might skyrocket in the process. Purity always has its price, I say.

3. EXERCISE

Exercise regularly. Whooee—that's almost as inspirational as "Drink water!" There is an overlooked factor here that sneaks up on the best of us. Exercise can actually kill you if you forget about the "regularly" part. If you want to take good care of yourself, put some effort into finding the right exercise for the way you live and what you truly enjoy. It might be that you aspire to be the roller blader from hell, tearing up the streets and sidewalks and looking slick in your hot roller blader stuff. But be real about this. And act your age. Knees wear out, you know. Elbows and shoulders do too. Are you starting to see rocking chair derbies in what I am saying? That is—the most excitement you dare have is to scoot a rocking chair across the floor faster than anyone else? Just be wise is all. And regular. If you actually can get in two or three tennis sessions a week, that's terrific. If you can't, don't make that your exercise, make it your entertainment. And go find something you can do two to three times a week for a half hour all year long. Amen.

4. SLEEP

Are you sleeping? I'm finding an alarming number of people are not getting good rest.

That would be eight *sound* hours of rest. Every night. Sleep deprivation occurs when you miss one good night of rest. After two missed nights, you should be a basket case.

So what can you do to make sure you're getting your critical z's? Prepare to sleep. Just falling into bed and conking out is rare. Good, restful sleep only comes when you're physically tired and emotionally calm.

Physically tired means that your muscles have been used enough to demand rest. If you want to get the kind of rest that allows your body and mind to fully recharge, *you must exercise*. There's no time for this, you say? Ask someone who routinely exercises at the end of their workday how they do it when everyone else feels too wiped out to do anything but collapse. They'll tell you that for the first few minutes they might still be feeling that stress drain we all know so well, but it disappears by the end of their workout. And they are also very relaxed. This is not hogwash. Go ahead and ask someone who works out or walks or does tai chi or yoga or swims or whatever.

Getting emotionally calm means putting aside all the pressing issues of the day. Writing a list of what you are going to do tomorrow works for

many people. Once you write everything down,
you can tell yourself that now that you have everything in writing, you don't have to lug around all
of your responsibilities through the night. You can
let them go. Then in the morning when you are
rested, you will be ready to take on all the items on
your list. Or the next morning you may discover
that what seemed so pressing when you were trying to get to sleep isn't such a big deal after all.

Remember those little "tucking in" rituals your
parents made for you? You still need some. Your
subconscious mind needs signals that say, "It is
now time to allow for relaxation and sleep." A cup
of warm milk or herbal tea, turning down the bed,
even an adult version of reading a story may be a
way to go. Just try not to let the story-reading go
on until two in the morning . . .

Here's a tucking in ritual I like:

Tucking In

➤ Fluff up your pillows and turn down the
covers on your bed. Make your bed look
inviting, a place to relax and sleep. This
eliminates televisions and computer
equipment.

➢ Now go to the kitchen and warm up a mug of milk or make a cup of soothing tea for yourself. There are several bed-time-type teas available on the market. Celestial Seasonings's "Tension Tamer" is a favorite of mine. If your supermarket doesn't have the good stuff, try checking out a health food store or a coffee specialty shop for more choices.

➢ While you are enjoying your milk or tea, make yourself a list of what is important to remember to do tomorrow. (I like to climb into bed to do this.) When you have finished your list, tell yourself that now that you have inventoried the important tasks for the next day, you can set them aside and rest. They won't be forgotten. They will be there in the morning for you to take on after you have had a good rest. Then set your list aside.

➢ Turn off the lights and settle yourself in bed. Here's how you settle. Lie on your back with your arms at your sides, close your eyes and take some slow, deep breaths. Imagine oxygen going all the way down to your toes as you inhale. Imagine all the tension and stress of the day flowing out as you exhale.

Continue taking slow, deep breaths and relax all of your muscles, starting at the top of your head and slowly working your way down to your toes. Focus on small sections of your body as you do this. Begin with relaxing your facial muscles, first gently focusing on your jaw. You might find yourself wanting to yawn. That's moving in the right direction. Now relax your temples, your eyes, your forehead. Focus on the back of your neck, relaxing all the muscles here. Then your shoulders. Move them slightly so they are in a more comfortable position. Then let the sense of relaxation flow all the way down your spine to your lower back. Let the muscles in your arms, starting at your shoulders, relax. Notice your hands. Let your hands relax, and your fingers, to the end of your fingertips. With your next breath, relax all the muscles in your chest, letting your body feel heavier and heavier. Now relax your stomach muscles. Let relaxation flow down your thighs, your calves, your feet, all the way to your toes.

Imagine yourself floating, drifting. Peaceful, relaxed.

You may fall asleep before you get to the end of your relaxation session. If you are awake when you get to the floating part, just keep going with the sensation. It should carry you off in a few minutes. Another thing you might want to try with this exercise is to have someone read it to you. Sort of an updated bedtime story. Or put it on tape yourself. If you do tape it, remember to read it very, very slowly in as soothing a voice as possible. Think of what it would take to gentle a frightened child.

Waking Up

If you find yourself waking up in the middle of the night, your first instinct might be to get tied up in knots about how you are awake when you should be sleeping. That usually succeeds in waking you up even more. If you can catch yourself before you hit the "I'm not asleep and it's three in the morn- ing!" panic button, getting back to sleep should be pretty easy. Natural rhythms of sleep which we all have, flow through the night, bringing you close to awakening at times and then dropping you back down into deep sleep. Go ahead and remind yourself of this, then turn over and let yourself drift for a bit.

What if you become fully alert? There are some things you can do to help set yourself up for your next sleep cycle. First on the list is the muscle relaxation exercise, starting with relaxing your toes, your feet, your ankles, your calves. Keep going all the way up. Take some time with this, and notice that focusing on one small section of your body at a time is the most effective method. It should work fine the other way around as well (starting with your eyes, mouth, jaw, neck, etc.). I have noticed that leg cramps can sometimes be the thing that wakes people up, so start with your toes if that's what has happened. If you are not out by the end of relaxing your muscles, top to bottom or bottom to top, play yourself some soothing music or a meditation tape. And let yourself relax.

There are times when stress levels get higher and you may find you are more restless at night. If that is what is happening for you, be ready to help yourself fall back asleep if you need it. Set up a tape on your tape player and put it by your bed. Have some water on your nightstand. Put a notepad and pen there, too. That way if an idea or a (ick!) worry is rolling around in your head, you can jot a note down on the pad and check back on it in the morning. And just knowing that you have prepared for the likelihood that you may awaken in the night may make the difference for you and help you sleep easier.

Getting Help

If you have done these things and you still aren't resting easily and well, it's time to get some help. You cannot compromise on sleep. Bodies do not work well without it, physically or emotionally. Have a physical examination and talk with your doctor about the sleep issue. It is not normal to consistently have trouble sleeping. If everything seems to be physically fine, do some checking into everything being emotionally fine as well. Get some support, so you can sleep. And be well.

chapter 6

Falling in Love with You

"**You've got personality!**" I'm not sure what it—personality—means, but no one seems to take it badly when this is said to them, and it has its very own song, so it must be something to shoot for, or to keep if you have it. And we all have it. It's a big part of how people identify us, our "personality." Our trademark, so much a part of our lives that it is how we recognize ourselves as well.

Then what's this we hear about a True Self? Is that our personality too? Somehow a True Self seems deeper, fuller, richer. Maybe we want both.

And how about our Real Self and our True Colors and . . . "Stop the Music, I Want to Get Off!" which you all probably want to do right now. Have I gotten carried away? Alright, I'll back up for a minute. Suppose that, without having a split personality, we all have a core self (the real you, your true colors, etc.) that is directly connected to our highest potential. The best, most soul-filled part of our being. And we also have a vehicle for the expression of that core self. For the sake of argument, let's call that personality.

Okay, which one, I ask you, is the cart and which one is the horse? This might sound like a chicken and egg kind of question, but it isn't. What I am meaning to suggest is that we *choose* our personality, the expression of our core. Or we can if we are aware that such a thing is possible. Perhaps this sounds nuts to you. Or pointless. You are who you are. After all, it worked for that great American hero, Popeye ("I yam what I yam!"). (And a veggie lover at that!)

Suppose for a minute that the way you express yourself in the world isn't necessarily written in stone. What if "That's just the way I am" and "I always act that way" are actually negotiable? Suppose that your personality—the way you have made yourself known to the world—is something you have constructed for yourself. And that the materials you built it with came out of what you heard and saw as you grew? Suppose you could decide to take a good look at those materials and make some choices about what you kept and what you threw out. Or you could decide to build in some things that you didn't have before. What would you change? How would you do such a thing? First of all, gradually. Overnight would throw people off and maybe get you committed. For me, that would mean having to live without lattes, and I'm just not ready for that. So I suggest approaching this whole thing with great care.

GETTING TO KNOW YOU

The first step is to take a close look at what your personality currently is. There is a fun way to do this: Fall in love with yourself. You've probably read some of the same self-help books that I have. Don't they all say that if you want to be happy, you have to love yourself? Not as an option. Essential. If you don't love yourself you'll never have what you're looking for, whatever it may be. So go ahead and fall in love. Go to that delightfully crazy state of being fascinated by everything about yourself.

Make it a little running dialogue in your head, noticing everything about you. Just like when you are totally, hopelessly in love with someone. Only do it for yourself. Taking notes (yes, actually writing

To know, know, know me is to love, love, love, me.

down all the things you notice, no matter how trivial) can also be helpful. The more details about your personality that you can capture at a conscious level, the more you have to work with when you're making choices about what you want to keep—and what makes more work for you than is worth having.

Let's say you've been at this for a while and you have a full notebook. It's time to make some choices. There is no right and wrong here; it's all about what works best for you. So if starting several projects at one time and knowing there isn't time to finish them all means you feel like you are constantly chasing your tail, you know that particular personality trait is one you don't need. Or maybe you love your ability to light so many fires at one time, and you decide to keep that trait as a hallmark of the way you are in the world. The critical thing here is to have an opportunity to compare your True Self (who you are beyond your personality) with what you are putting out and choosing what fits best for you.

Here's an exercise you might find helpful:

1. You need a notebook or journal for this. (Are you beginning to notice that *Full Tilt Living* gives you lots of opportunities to

make use of all those books with blank pages you have lying about?) On a daily (yes, daily!) basis jot down one thing you have noticed about yourself. Notice things that you would notice about a new friend—how great you are at problem solving, what perfect coffee you make, how well you dance, what a great swimmer you are, how organized you are. Notice things that don't fall in the "Aren't I wonderful?" category too. You want it all here. One month of this should be enough. If you've become thoroughly infatuated with yourself, make it two.

2. Get yourself a highlighter. Highlight what you like about you. These are the keepers. Now take a look at what is not highlighted. You are probably not happy with yourself for having the unhighlighted traits. It's time to be big-hearted and forgive yourself for them and move on.

3. Make a new list with two columns. In the first column, write down your unhighlighted traits. In the column next to it, make a positive statement of how you can change. For example, if in column one you have written, "I am late with my electricity

bill," next to it you could write, "I pay my electricity bill on the tenth of every month."

4. Use your list of positive statements to reprogram. Cut the list in half lengthwise so you now have only your new positive statements. Now put them somewhere you can read them. Spend the next month reviewing them daily—yes, daily! Review means read them over, not necessarily pound them into your head. You just need a light reminder of what they are for the autopilot part of you to get the message.

A PINCH OF THIS, A DASH OF THAT

How about additions you may want to make? Now that you are aware of what the mix in your personality is, you might also be aware of, shall we say, the gaps. How about not terrorizing yourself with a long list of things you aren't that you want to be. This is no time to fall out of love with yourself. Give yourself credit for where you have gotten so far without even knowing that you have been doing it.

Take a long serious look at what you feel you want to add to your personality. Maybe being kind to dogs isn't such a great thing after all. Make a few choices. Make an "A" list. Choose one item from this list, write it on a card. Remember those 3 x 5 cards people used before they had computers? They still carry them at the stationery store. Buy yourself a pack, in color if you like. Starting with "I am . . . " write a statement from your "A" list and stick it on your mirror. Really! Read it to yourself every day for a month as you look in the mirror.

Admire yourself when you say the words, imagining how great you will feel about yourself when you recognize this new trait built into your personality. Then at the end of the month, switch. If you have a streak of organization in your personality, you might want to make yourself a set of cards with one item from your "A" list on each card so you can be ready to change the card on your mirror at the beginning of a new month.

Use the cards until you are happy with the results. Remember to switch them so the one up on the mirror doesn't just become a blur in the background.

I did another version of this little card trick one time several years ago. I wanted to sort of pep myself up during the day without anyone noticing, so I took a pad of blank Post-it notes, the smallest, most unobtrusive size. This time I didn't actually write on them. I just held them in my hand as I focused on thinking positive things about myself. (It was a little like I was using invisible ink.) Then, during the day when I felt I needed it, I would pick up a pad and hold it for a few moments. It worked very well. I still harbor a certain fondness for those little notes. I admit this to no one.

Here's a summary of the card trick you can use as you check out who you are and how you want to be in the world.

The Me I Want to Be

- Write brief statements about which traits you would like to have. Things that didn't show up as you wrote in your getting-to-know-you journal and that you wish had. Go on and on. Get them all out!

- Take out your highlighter again and select the ones that are the most important to you.

- Take each highlighted trait and write it on a card (one per card) starting with, "I am . . ."

- Stick one card on your mirror. Every time you look in the mirror, read the card to yourself. Admire yourself when you say the words, imagining how great you will feel about yourself when you recognize this new trait built into your personality. At the end of a month, switch to a new card.

Something that might happen when you begin making personality choices is having your personality become more fluid, maybe more adaptable to the situations and personalities it is encountering. It does, of course, still have its source in your highest, core being and carries the spark and colors of your true self. Someone you can love being in love with.

chapter 7

Change: Roaring Out of the Rut

*C*hange happens. **All the time.** We often welcome it. It's what we long for when the winter gets too long and too cold. It comes with new choices, fresh ideas. It signals that we can become more, better, happier. But it can also cook up a lot of pressure.

For example, I'd be willing to wager that it's usually February before you use all the great new stuff you got over the holidays. Because you have to make room for the new stuff in all directions: physically, mentally (which may be the toughest—those tiny instruction books with their odd little diagrams can take hours to translate), emotionally. New stuff means change. They may be changes that are welcome. But still, they ask something of us, of our time, of our focus.

Other things also come along that mean change. People come and go in our lives, and that makes for change. Jobs change, sometimes when we're looking for that to happen and sometimes not. Styles have a quirky way of changing for me just when I'm getting the hang of the last one that came along.

All of this change business comes with a built-in price tag: a change on the outside doesn't come without a change on the inside.

Having a feel for what that inside change will ask of you can make for some real mountains of stress. And that can stop a perfectly useful change in its tracks. Ever been to a meeting where everyone in the room is sitting with their arms crossed and staring at nothing in particular? There's a good chance that change is in the air and nobody likes it! Yup. We actually do respond to change, that lovely, freeing, exhilarating opportunity to embrace new and unexplored territory with FEAR.

How do we get past putting on the brakes when change comes on the scene? Taking our internal temperature can be very helpful. We all have a personalized version of, to put it bluntly, shutting

Change on the
outside
doesn't come
without change
on the
inside.

down. Now don't get embarrassed by this, but think back on how it is that you do it, step by step. I usually start with a visible stiffening and then sort of holding my breath. After that I can hear a little voice inside my head shrieking, "NO! NO! NO!" Really. I'm relieved no one else can hear it. That's when I know my internal temperature is at the breaking point, as in READY TO SHUT DOWN.

But hey, if you can see it starting to happen, you can choose what you do next. I suggest you start by letting yourself have a time-out. You probably will be doing this anyway in one form or other—remember that stuff about arm-crossing and that "not interested" look? That's it. Recognize your time-out for what it is and let it help you get across the "Oh, no!!" chasm. Use it to take a moment to be compassionate with that part of you that wants to keep you from harm by staying as far away as possible from the lurking dangers inherent in the "C" word.

MAKING ROOM FOR CHANGE

Now that you've acknowledged and honored where you stand in relation to a change, what's next? Make room. Ask your self (the squealing, shaking part) to take a closer look at what might be good about change. Consider the possibility that the change could be an okay part of you, not the enemy it was looking like when you first noticed it.

The door should be open a crack by now, so let the good stuff in. Let that playful, unrestricted, creative part of yourself be in charge. It will be there for you once your brakes are off. Enjoy all the possibilities your change brings with it. Feel the expansion it creates! Enjoy the moment! Dive in!

ROARING OUT OF THE RUT

Cake. Space Hog. Fine Young Cannibals.

I read that on a billboard recently. For a minute it looked like a menu written backwards. An ad for a new restaurant? An ad for a record store, actually. As I wrote down the names of the recording groups, I thought of what a fresh, inventive, energy-efficient use of language they had. So much communicated with one word, so innovative in the way the words hung together. Another dimension of reality, really. I could say, "Not my form of relating, not my vision." Unless I would be willing to stretch my boundaries to make room for them. And why not? What would it be like to be totally surrounded with sounds that are not the ones I know? Not forming a judgment about whether they fit for me or if I liked them. Just giving them a whirl. Swishing them around in my personal space, but not necessarily making them a permanent addition. And if I could do *that*, what else might I want to invite into my little emotional safety zone?

After all, do I want to spend the rest of my life just sticking with the things that are comfortable? We all seem to get into the habit of repeating the way we do things. We choose "favorites" and then narrow our vision so we don't even see the possibility of choice any longer. I'm not talking about candy bars here (nothing can take the place of Snickers in my heart) but about closing doors and shutting out opportunities just by hanging on to a "favorite" way of doing things. But recognizing an opportunity to move out of our comfort zones and making use of that opportunity can be a way to make sure we're keeping those doors open and letting life be a little richer than it might otherwise be.

MOVING OUTSIDE YOUR COMFORT ZONE

Anyone interested in joining me in a little experiment? This is how it works: You use your own "backyard" for this, so it's really easy to do.

Notice when you are encountering something in your everyday life that bumps into your comfort zone. Anything will do. The way someone eats in a restaurant that is different from the way you do, someone else's choice of music, a magazine whose point of view or subject matter makes squealing noises begin to come out of your throat when you see it, a movie that you would never dream of seeing.

Now take a mental deep breath, or maybe an actual one, and dive in! Invite "it" into your personal space. Dip your bread in the sauce, change radio stations, buy the magazine, sit through the entire film with your eyes open.

Go ahead and let it be an adventure! Savor the differences. Feel the impact it has on your idea of how the world should be.

Try this more than once if you like. And maybe watch yourself as you function outside of your comfort zone. Does your sense of curiosity expand or contract? Is it exciting to dump yourself into foreign territory, or is it more or less terrifying? Or do you just completely numb out and feel almost nothing happening?

So what is behind this offer to taste what it would be like to expand your world into someone else's? A couple of things, actually. For starters, giving yourself something else to focus on for a while is a great way to move out of feeling a little down and out of sorts. Just turning your attention to something completely outside yourself can give you a vacation from the daily stuff that may be wearing on you. And then you come back from your mini adventure feeling a little more vital, maybe, a little less ground down. Or you might find that issues that seemed so overwhelming aren't so hard to deal with after all.

CHOOSING CHANGE

The way I see it, you can choose your changes or you can let them choose you. And as exhilarating as being swept along may be, I like to have some say in where the tides take me. So here's a way to get ready for changes and maybe do some directing so you get the change you want when the opportunity comes along.

Keep a Dreams Book

➢ Keep an eye out for ideas that pop into your head, especially the ones that you give that instant "Hey, that would be great" response. Watch out for the backlash—"Okay, it may be great, stupid, but it is NOT POSSIBLE." That's just the protective side of your personality trying to keep you from a painful fall. Just send a thank-you to your protective side for wanting to take care of you and go on with your dream program.

➢ Write the idea down in your Dreams Book and save some pages for it. You are going to want to come back to it as more ideas come to you. I want to mention here that there is no limit to the number of dream ideas you write in your book. The more you have, the more you can choose from later on.

➢ Give your Dreams Book a little structure. This is going to be different from working with goals. With a goal, you have already committed to reaching it. With a dream, you are going to give yourself room to play. It may never even leave your Dreams

Book. First, think about how you would like the specifics of your dream to look. If it's a thing, like a car or a place to live or a stereo system, go for features, colors, sizes, models you have seen and like. If it's not a thing but rather a skill or a relationship or an event, bring up all of the things you can imagine it to be like. Write all of this down. Call this section "How my ____ looks." Keep in mind that you can revisit this and change it any time you like.

➤ Then find out what this dream means to you. Write down why you want it. Write what it will bring to you. Call this section "What my ____ means to my life."

➤ Place your dream in time. Some things that seem immediate when you first think of them are really things you aren't ready for right away. Know when you do this step that time is yours to play with. Call this section "When I will have my ____."

You might want your Dreams Book to have a scrapbook format with pictures and articles you find. You might want to do some drawing in it. You might want to store it on a disc. It's your chance to be totally individual and free of any need to do anything other than to play with the possibilities of changes.

If you would feel more comfortable having a "Why?" for your Dreams Book, I'm happy to supply a few. You are building a new habit with it. You are becoming a person who can live with the possibility of constant change and enjoy it. You are also getting to know what is important to you on a more conscious level. This means that when one of those opportunities to change comes along, you'll be much more prepared to jump on it because you have been practicing recognizing which changes can benefit you. You can, to say it another way, find it much easier to "go for it."

One more thing; when you're ready to change one of your dreams to a goal, it will be simple to set up. Add a target date and list the steps to take to get there. You're on your way!

chapter 8
Kicking the Habits

We all have an **uncountable** number of habits. Good, bad, inherited, thought up on our own. Think of what life would be like without them: you would have to wonder every morning if it would be better to feed the cat or shower first, decide whether or not to read the paper with your coffee, ask yourself if you want butter on your toast (or maybe a bagel would be better), think about what to say to people you meet on the way to work. And just imagine how many more decisions you would encounter before you even made it to lunch! The same ones over and over every day!

Habits are starting to look pretty great in the face of this. You can make your choice about how you are going to do things once and you never have to think about it again.

For that matter, stuff gets decided once and for all for you by your parents before you are even old enough to figure out what it was you were choosing. That's where those "always" things come from. In my family, we always had bacon and eggs for Sunday breakfast. We always polished our shoes on Saturday night. We always brushed with Colgate, and we never spat out the car window (after that first time, anyway—it was a contest to see how far it could go, and my sister won).

"Okay, okay," you say. "Don't sweat the small stuff. Who cares what kind of toothpaste I use?" It's not the toothpaste I'm talking about. It's just knowing that programming has happened.

The "always" things that seem set in conrete can also come from choices you made so early in your life that you don't remember them.

I had a client who discovered that the reason she overate stemmed from an experience she had as a toddler. The aunt who had taken her in when her mother died saw choices as something adults made for children. A basic part of good child care. The message my client heard at the tender age of one-and-one-half years old was that she was not allowed to decide what or how much she would eat. My client, even before she could speak clearly, had a completely different idea. It was, "I choose for myself." She had been belligerently stuffing herself to prove her point ever since. Eating more than her fill became a habit. It became one of those "always" things.

Consider this: You can take something that you thought you were stuck with for the rest of your life and toss it out. It doesn't have to be an "always." It is something you choose to make a habit. You can make another choice. One you like better. If programming can happen, it can be undone. If you want, that is.

To change a habit takes focus. It takes planning and practice. Is this starting to smack of training camp? Okay, I fess up. I am sending you to training camp. You want to change a habit, you have to go into training. Because habits you don't want cannot get kicked just like that. Not news to you, I am sure.

A habit you don't want anymore has to be replaced. You need to choose a new, better habit to take its place. So you don't stop eating in order to lose weight, you train in healthier eating habits. And you don't give up cigarettes in order to stop smoking, you choose healthier practices to replace the smoking.

I will say this another way. The habit you now have is giving you something. If you try to just dump it, you will really miss it. You will probably miss it so much that you will go back to it.

If you replace your habit with something similar that is better for you, you will begin to lock onto that new thing instead. It will come to be the "always" thing that you do. This is not to say that you will immediately drop chocolate eclairs for a cup of peppermint tea. Or find a walk break as satisfying as a cigarette break. This is where going into training comes in. And here's how you can train in a new habit.

HABIT TRAINING

1. **Find a coach.** You can be your own, but that is doing things the hard way. I'm going to give a big plug to hypnotherapy here. It is, in my experience, a powerful tool for habit change. There are other programs that have had good results for people as well. Choose one that has regular meetings, with emphasis on supporting your progress.

2. **Put your goal down in writing.** Be as concrete as you can. Include a date for

reaching your goal. If you want to drop weight, write down your ideal size and when you will be that size, for example. (Be realistic with this. If you are never going to be a size eight with your bone structure, do not make size eight your ideal.) If you are eliminating smoking, make a statement like, "I will be free of cigarettes by . . ." Give yourself a time line that you have a reasonable shot at reaching. Set yourself up for success, not failure.

3. **Post your goal.** It is one of your training tools, and you want to have it in sight. In your planner, on the refrigerator, on your mirror, on the dashboard, on your computer screen, in your palm pilot, on your phone.

4. **Write your action plan.** This is where replacing old patterns with new ones comes into play. You are going to build this by making a *complete* list of the times and places you do the "always" thing that you are eliminating. Now you are going to be creative—for every one of those items on your list, write a new activity. If you have a cigarette on your way to work in the morning, give yourself something else to

do that is similar to your old activity. Taking out a stick of gum and unwrapping it can work as a replacement for getting that cigarette out of the pack. If you usually light up just before you sit down to work, try filling the gap by giving your hands something else to do. A quick hand massage works. And let yourself be a little wacky when you make the new list. Make the replacements fun. I can see the possibility of taking up the harmonica. It is impossible to eat or smoke when you're playing. Pretty soon your friends will be asking for requests. Or they could start buying you doughnuts or offering you one of their cigarettes to get you to put it away.

5. **Chart your progress.** Choose a day of the week for your review. On that day share your results with your coach if you have one. Congratulate yourself on your success. Look at where your trouble spots occurred and adjust your action plan. Now dive into a new week. If the week before was really rocky, let it be over and let it go. If it was great and you hit every mark, let that wave carry you into the new week.

6. **Get a little obsessed.** You know how it is when you buy a new car and suddenly you see every car on the road is the same model as yours? And your car starts jumping off the page in magazine ads? You might start telling people how great your car is. You read articles about it. You buy special stuff to clean it. You find excuses to take people places. Yeah. Obsessed. So get obsessed about your new habit. Go to the bookstore and buy books about it. Look for ideas in magazines and on the Net to support your new habit. Share tips with people who are working on the same goal.

7. **Add new activities.** Back up your habit change with additions to your daily routine that make your new choices happen more often.

   If it's eating patterns you are working on, buy the best fresh fruit you can find and have it in every place you like to snack—on the kitchen counter, at work, at a friend's when you visit.

   If you are eliminating cigarettes, take a "walk break" and inhale consciously and deeply, focusing on how great your lungs feel when you treat them to fresh air. Make your walk last the same amount of time

that it would take you to smoke a cigarette. If you are adding more exercise,
become extra aware of opportunities to
stretch, take short walks, walk the "long
way," take the stairs.

If your new focus is to take more care of
your well-being, enjoy a series of small
events during the day—a thirty second
deep breathing session; a favorite view; a
long, slow drink of spring water.

8. **Take classes.** Exercise classes and meditation classes can really enrich your training
regimen. An exercise class will help you
lose weight, build muscles, and burn more
calories every day. It will also reduce stress.
Did you know that sweating, aside from
letting the world know how you are
knocking yourself out, releases toxins that
are created by stress? To say nothing of the
chemicals your body produces when you
exercise that make you feel terrific.
Exercise classes can also give you some
alternatives for smoking. For example, you
can easily do a couple of yoga stretches in
the middle of the day when it feels like it's
time for a cigarette. Meditation increases
your ability to focus and not get pulled off
track when some juicy thing dripping of

calories catches your eye on a menu, or you absently reach for your cigarettes. And it will take you completely out of stress. While we're at it, low-fat cooking classes can be great as well. Better food choices, a break from stress-filled routines, something new to do with your hands when you start looking for a cigarette.

9. **The final review.** When you arrive at the date you assigned to reach your goal, give yourself a final review. Notice that there is a huge difference between evaluating life goals and work goals. If you get to the final review date for the life goal you selected and you achieved what you expected, you are probably going to congratulate yourself on a job well done. If you haven't, you can't just assign someone else to your project or fire yourself. What you can do is acknowledge what you have accomplished. If you made changes to how you live that are better for you, you have put yourself on the road to having what you want. Take a good look at what worked and what didn't. Now build on what you have accomplished so far and set up a new plan. Because it's not over until

it's over; it's not over until the fat lady sings; where there's life there's hope; you'll never walk alone; and all roads lead to Rome. (I was running out of platitudes at the end). In other words, you can always give yourself another chance. And you will do better at reaching your goal the second time with all the experience you gained from the first time to back you up.

chapter 9
Endings

So you have gone ahead and revved up your emotional engine to rock out of a rut. You have embraced change, taken it in like a long lost friend. The end of a change should be a breeze then, a cakewalk, or at least the icing. You've already made room for the change, you know how it feels and where it fits. It doesn't surprise you when you get up in the morning anymore.

But endings themselves can be the most gargantuan kinds of change. Like when you finally graduate (and notice how many people are relieved that you have!). But you find yourself wanting one last cup of disgusting cafeteria coffee, or feeling empty without the familiar pressure of too many papers to write and not enough time to write them. Or you trade in your used-to-be dream car for the really true car of your dreams that you thought could never be yours. And you worry about who will buy your old car and have to wiggle the key in the ignition before the lock will release and if they will understand that personality doesn't just come to a car overnight. Endings might feel like part of you is getting left behind, that you are losing something you can't get back . . .

And when those endings involve things that aren't your choice, especially when they involve people, the effect can be like a bomb exploding in your chest. I don't believe we've been properly wired for that. Nests empty. Best friends move to the other side of the continent. Good things for them. Good for you as well, you say. But still there is a hollow left after the celebration, like a crater in the earth. Unfamiliar and unwelcome.

Some endings are the kind that mean there is no way to fill the hollow: no school to revisit, no trip to the new place with new friends to meet. The dimension of loss can take on some huge proportions. At the extreme end of the spectrum, what we often see as the end of all endings, is death.

I had a friend who was diagnosed with a disease that would end his life and take away his world and the people he had filled it with. He had a pair of brass cymbals from his marching band days that he took out and marched with through his neighborhood, clashing them as he went. When he tried to march through Safeway, they took the cymbals away from him. By then he felt he had made his point. He had announced to himself and the hearing world that he was entering into new territory; he was encountering loss.

It's personal terrain, loss. I don't pretend to have a map through it. I have picked up a few pointers along the way that I'd like to share with you. I hope they will help make a completely insane situation take on a few moments of clarity and maybe peace as you work your way through your loss.

NOTICE THE BREATHING SPACES

What may at first appear to be a very dark, bottomless pit doesn't remain bottomless forever. Just for the moments that it seems bottomless. And those moments are just that. They won't stop being bottomless even if you tell them to. At the beginning of a loss, these moments will be longer. You might find that they begin to be interspersed with bright moments that seem almost out of place in contrast. You might even want to pull away from these moments because they seem trivial, even flippant, in the face of your loss.

We each need
to chart our
personal
loss terrain.

They are not to be taken lightly, however. They are holding the seeds to your healing. So root out as many of them as you can and enjoy the small oases they create. Even a bowl of cornflakes with ice cold milk can make a world of difference. Or getting caught up in the flight of birds that suddenly brings life and movement to your landscape.

I have a friend who tells how she found herself walking numbly though the park after hearing of her ex-partner's death. She was stopped by the sight of a pheasant on the path. The encounter gave her a little breathing space. She is still grateful for that moment.

LET IT OUT OF YOUR BODY

Loss can be physically painful. The explosion in your chest, for instance. And it can seem to weigh on you. Grief does these things. I remember my mom turning to me as we sat in my parents' car after my sister's funeral and saying in her usual unvarnished way, "The first three days are the hardest. After that, it's easier." Yes. The physical part does ease.

I've found being able to weep can help this along. It is also a better choice than busting things up.

Exercise is also critical as loss is processed. Curling up in a ball in the dark, which is what you may want to do more than anything else, cuts off your oxygen supply and actually increases depression. You need circulation and light. What I am suggesting here may sound very cold and mechanical and disrespectful of the depth of your grief. How could a little fresh air possibly contend with the load you are carrying? Amazingly well, in my experience.

YOU WILL WANT TO ASSIGN BLAME

There is one part of making it through a loss that may take you a bit by surprise; you are going to want to blame someone for it. You may be totally irrational about this. Your survival skills may have you looking to flush out the enemy and stomp it. Make it hurt just as much as it hurt you. Like wanting to destroy the car involved in the loss, or execute your ex, or sue the hospital, or slowly strangle your boss.

There might not even be a rational link between what you have lighted on as your enemy and the source of your grief. It might be a part of the event, but not in any way responsible. Logically speaking, that is.

I'm suggesting you watch for what or who you choose to blame, because you are going to do it. When you do, acknowledge that you are feeling flooded by hatred and ready for revenge. Do not take revenge. Do not file law suits or get the name of the guy who said he'd be happy to break your brother-in-law's legs. Know that what you are experiencing is grief. Grieve.

PROMISE TO DO SOME GOOD

Promise yourself that when you have reached a point further down the line in your grieving process, you will do some good. You can think of it as finding a way to make sure someone else does not have to hurt in the way you have. Great causes have come out of just such passionate wishes for justice to be done. MADD (Mothers Against Drunk Drivers) comes to mind. I'm sure you know many more.

KEEP THE EXITS CLEAR

Make some doorways for your loss to flow through. If you have experienced a death, there are lots of opportunities for this. Wearing clothing in colors that carry the symbol of grief, lighting candles, burning incense, gathering to pray and sing and to say your farewells, accepting the flowers and cards and food and words from people who care about you. Choose the ones that work best for you. These things are, in a way, a resource for you. Take full advantage. It has long been known that flowers can have an actual positive physical effect and that the light of a fire warms us in more than one way.

If you are facing a loss without the benefit of the support of your community, you are still very much in need of those doorways for loss to flow through. You're going to have to improvise. You can use the traditional forms as a template and adapt them to fit what is happening for you. One major difference is that the outside world will probably not be pitching in to help here. Hallmark isn't putting out too many cards expressing sympathy over the loss of your job. The death of a relationship isn't a big one for them, either. After all, you could really get on the wrong side of someone wishing them well on their divorce when they don't see much "well" about it. Counting on phone calls may be more productive. This is one thing you can put to very good use. Talking about loss is definitely another doorway. So is writing, but be careful about sending letters. I'd say writing to yourself is the most productive. Give yourself flowers. Listen to your music. Light candles, one for what you have lost, one for yourself, one for every heart your loss has touched. Sit in their light. Let them speak for you.

KNOW YOUR OWN RHYTHM

One last thought, and for this we turn to the kitchen. Where you will find an onion. If you peel off the outer layer of the onion, you will find another layer underneath. If you peel that, guess what you find. That is not far from what you might find with loss. It has layers and makes you weep.

I may be veering dangerously toward silly, but it's true. Loss does have layers. You can only get through them one at a time. It calls for patience with yourself, because it won't be over when you want it to be over. It will be over when you have finished healing. And that is a very personal thing.

When you have finished with the onion peeling and have had a thoroughly good cry, put your onion in a pot with a chicken and some other good things. Let it simmer. Let it turn into something to nourish you and give you strength. Maybe that's how chicken soup got started . . .

For those of you who like to work from a list, here is one with the suggestions I have made, as

well as some new ideas, to help you navigate
through a loss.

➢ Get on the phone and call someone. Talk
about how you feel, if you can. If the
words won't come out, tell them what has
happened. Let them share your grief for a
few minutes. Thank them.

➢ Take yourself out for a walk. Make it a
walk that gives you room to be quiet if you
need that. Take your walk in a place that
gives you room to scream or weep if you
need that. Remember to breathe deeply.

➢ Light three candles: one for what you have
lost, one for yourself, and one for every
heart your loss has touched. Light them in
your home. Light them in your church.

➢ Go to a flower shop. Stand among the
flowers. Make a bouquet for yourself.
Choose bright, uplifting colors. Pick flowers with fragrance. Take them home and
put them in the room where you live the
most. Be near them as often as you can.

➢ Play your music. It has a way of opening
the inner doors to the places where you
hold grief and letting it flow out. Make a

date with yourself to listen at least once a
week.

➤ Begin a search for causes or organizations
that you see as places to put your energy
when you are ready to do some good. Start
a collection of brochures and contacts.
Promise yourself that when you are ready,
you will choose one to support in memory
of your loss.

➤ Make yourself a steaming pot of good
homemade soup.

chapter 10
Talking Hearts—
the Gutsy Choice

Do you remember that line in the Christmas carol that mentions "hearts aglow?" Or have I gotten it confused with logs on the hearth? Either way, I have to say it's a pretty inspired thought, hearts glowing.

Actually, some very old traditions from the wise people in the eastern part of our blue marble have a lot to say about hearts glowing. I don't know how much influence those folks had on our holiday songs, but I remember from Christmas stories told to me in childhood that they did get in on the act in Bethlehem some time around January. At that point, as the story goes, most of the excitement was over. I'm sure they were sorry to have missed the angels and the trumpets. I have to hand it to them for their excellent sense of direction and keen ability to star gaze, however.

These wise people from the East knew that there is such a thing as a certain kind of energy that emanates from the heart, and energies that emanate from other "centers" as well. In this Eastern tradition, these centers are often called chakras (pronounced shock-raws). You can see how tough that would be to work into a carol. "Shock-raws on fire" certainly doesn't speak to me. But they do have this whole thing worked out with some very nice diagrams available in most Eastern meditation publications. The one often used is an outline of a person seated in lotus position (looking incredibly serene for a human pretzel) with stylized flower shapes at each chakra.

The Western world isn't entirely clueless about these energy centers, though it is sort of hit-or-miss from my experience. The heart center gets a fair amount of play. Here are a few examples that I have seen crop up in common usage: "They opened their hearts to them," "heartfelt," "hard-hearted Hannah, the Vamp of Savannah," "It touched my heart," and "Can you find it in your heart?" That one usually comes up around asking for forgiveness.

There is another center that gets a lot of mention; the center located in the solar plexus. That would be about halfway between the bottom of your rib cage and your belly button. Things said about this one would be; "It hit me right in the gut" (figuratively, of course) and "It gave me a queasy feeling in the pit of my stomach."

The throat center gets some notice, too. Think about the expression "The words got stuck in my throat." That's the result of the throat muscles contracting when we find it hard to say something. Your throat center, which is involved with energy relating to speaking your truth, as New Age types like to say, does seem be the route for expressing the thoughts of your inner wisdom. Your throat muscles can try to put on the brakes if you are feeling uncomfortable about what you are about to say.

START WITH WHAT YOU KNOW

Because I'm guessing you've had the most experience with the heart and the solar plexus centers, we'll be taking a closer look at these two for now. They seem to work almost opposite each other; if your focus is on the heart, your solar plexus energy doesn't seem to be in play, and vice versa. When we have that twist-in-the-gut sensation going on in the solar plexus, we'll usually find our heart center has blinked out.

Okay, I can hear you from here. You're asking, but can we actually make a conscious choice to have our heart glowing, or to not have that clenching feeling come at us when we feel threatened? Isn't this the stuff that just happens automatically? The truth is, once you know that you have chakras to work with, you can.

The challenge is that most people automatically match energy type for energy type—heart for heart, gut for gut. That's pretty nice with heart energy, but if someone hits you with a bolt of survival/kill-or-be-killed energy from his or her solar plexus, it takes a bit of concentration to remember that you have a choice about what you do with it. And getting all fired up with that "defend the castle" solar plexus heat can be kind of fun. The pull is very strong from this center. But the results are just not as good as what you get from your heart center. Insights into solutions aren't there in the solar plexus. The need to defend yourself at all costs certainly is, and the result of taking care of yourself "at all costs" can wind up giving you a lot of damage control to do afterwards. That doesn't happen if you operate from the heart center.

Do I hear mutterings about being turned into a wuss if you shift out of the solar plexus and into the

Insight lives in our hearts.

heart center? Some feelings of letting people walk
all over you? What I say is, don't knock it until
you've tried it. There is tremendous power in the
heart center. You can actually get a sense of being
in the middle of the fray without being touched by
it. And will probably find that you won't need the
usual recovery time when it's over. You actually feel
lifted when you operate from heart center energy,
not drained and smashed as you might after a bout
of letting your solar plexus roar.

OPENING THE HEART

But we're getting ahead of ourselves. What I'd like
you to do first is just practice locating your heart
energy and playing with it. This is an opportunity
to be creative as you develop this skill. You might
want to start by centering on your heart in meditation. Once you have gotten quiet, notice your
breathing. Let your breathing become slow so you
can follow it as you inhale and exhale. As you
inhale, imagine breathing into your heart. As you
exhale, imagine your heart energy flowing out. Let
the room fill with your heart energy as you continue to inhale and exhale slowly and deeply. Now
just imagine focusing in and "sitting" in your heart
center. Make use of your imagination muscles to
experience the energy here. It might have a sense

of flow, or it might rotate, or have some other physical sense. It might have color. It might pulse with your heart rhythm. It may appear to have chambers, like your heart.

Hold this only as long as it is enjoyable for you. If the energy seems to fade, or if you find you have to put effort into this, it's time to let it go. Come back to this "heart space" at other times during the day. Whenever you think of it, just touch in briefly.

When you become comfortable with this, try touching into your "heart space" while you are listening to someone. You'll probably notice this new heart energy you are creating affecting your interaction, making it smoother, or perhaps you might find yourself tuning in to the "heart" of the person you're with.

Once you've got the hang of this, try communicating from your heart center. Locate the sense of your heart however you usually do. I find that putting my attention on the physical area of my heart can easily get me there. Now just keep that focus in the back of your mind while you are talking with someone. Make it a light touch, sort of floating on your heart center. Watch what happens. Notice differences. Play with this a few times until you are comfortable.

Now put it to the test. The next time you come upon a situation when you're feeling a little challenged (I said *a little*—save the big stuff for later), like when somebody cuts in front of you in a lunch line or your phone rings when you need to concentrate on a project, check in with yourself and see if your energy is focused in your solar plexus. If a little voice inside you is mumbling some unprintable stuff, or you stop yourself just before you give someone a rightly earned shove, you have just the moment we're looking for.

The idea is to move out of your solar plexus and into your heart center. You might experience some resistance to doing this. At this point, I often feel sort of glued to my solar plexus. The shift might be easier if you aim your imagination at your heart center. Give it a try. Then just let things flow from there.

When you're at the point where you're doing these little exercises without much effort, try one more thing. Start noticing which of these two centers you normally operate from. Then notice when it is that you tend to gravitate toward one or the other. Knowing your own patterns and autopilot-type choices well can help you make the most of this new skill.

It is commonly held that a new habit takes thirty days to take hold. When you've passed the thirty-day mark with this, go ahead and try it on big stuff.

And remember to be patient with yourself as you work with it. Even angels have been known to throw a lightning bolt or two.

If you want to continue to play with this heart center idea, here's a list for you list folks:

1. Introduce yourself to your heart center. Find a quiet place and do your centering exercise, gently following your breath in and out. Let your attention gather where you imagine your heart to be. Continue your breathing exercise as you "sit" in your heart center. Notice what the energy seems like in this center. Does it have a color, a shape? Does it move?

2. Put yourself into your heart center during the day. Touch in when you have a quiet moment. Play with putting yourself in your heart center when things are really rolling. Notice if the energy here changes as your activity changes.

3. Try a conversation with someone while you are in your heart center. Hold the center lightly, sort of in the back of your

Be patient
with yourself.

mind, both while you are listening and while you are speaking. See if you can hold an awareness of both your heart center and the heart center of the person you are with. Notice the difference between an interaction with and without heart centers.

4. Play with moving out of your solar plexus and into your heart center. Wait for a moment when you sense that your solar plexus energy has been activated—survival instincts arising over something mildly challenging is a good place to start—and imagine yourself shifting up into your heart center as you deal with the issue. When it seems to be relatively easy to make the shift on smaller things, try it out with more critical issues. You want to start with things like the guy who can't get your coffee order right and then move up to having a bomb dropped on you by your boss or your best friend. Or maybe the other way around, depending on how you feel about coffee.

5. See where you normally head—heart or solar plexus—when things come up for you. Use this new understanding of how

you ordinarily operate as a way to get ahead of your solar plexus wave and know when you will want to make a shift to your heart center.

6. Keep in mind that the average time to develop a new habit and have it seem second nature to you is thirty days. Give yourself some opportunities for trial and error. And remember, you are not doing this heart center thing to turn into a wuss, you're doing it to be more clearheaded and to access your higher, stronger, more creative self in a crunch. After all, Superman wore his "S" over his heart . . .

chapter 11
Picking up Cues

What I love about movies is that movies have bad-guy music and good-guy music, and uh-oh!-something-terrible-is-about-to-happen music, and nothing-could-be-more-wonderful music, and this-is-really-funny music, and here-is-the-love-of-your-life music. You can't miss knowing what is going on just by listening.

It probably all started with the organists in those first movie houses wanting to make things a little more exciting. At this point, it means that you can sit through a really cheesy movie with your eyes shut and not miss a thing. I'm a little bitter about this. I suppose I could just stop going to cheesy movies and drop the whining. But it won't help. My issue is that I want to have a little sound system of my own. I don't necessarily need a full brass section. A couple of violins and a trumpet would probably cover it. I just want what any movie, even a low-budget one, has. I want cues. Not that I'm expecting to have an ensemble following me around. I was thinking an inner-sound system would be the way to go. So if someone was saying something I should pay attention to, I would hear a trumpet. Or if I was about to walk into trouble, the violins could play something tense-sounding. Like that.

I have figured out that I'm not getting that. It's not equipment that I was issued and that's the end of it. No amount of whining is changing things. So I've come up with a cueing system of my own.

THE ERASER

The first step in creating our own inner-cue system is to recognize the high level of static we have going on in our heads. You know, that continuous buzz of half-formed thoughts or bits and pieces of worrisome things that pop up.

My favorites are stuff like:

- How many more days until the first of the month?

- Where will I put the four people coming for the weekend when I only have one futon?
- Is that a patrol car driving behind me, and who says you can't hold a cell phone and drive at the same time?!!

Who could hear anything through that, right?

My method to clear the lines of all this useless stuff is to use The Eraser. Here's how it works. When one of these beauties comes up (and I am incredibly good at creating some real whoppers), I don't ignore it, I turn it in a positive direction. Like "When the first of the month comes, I'll be ready to pay my bills," or "There's plenty of room for people to sleep here. Nobody expects this to be a four-star hotel," or "I'll just make this phone call later." The positive idea cancels out the negative idea, and I get clear air space.

If you're giving The Eraser a try, expect it to take some time before you stop making static. The drama that goes into making up stuff to scare yourself can be a little tough to let go of. The Eraser works for me partially because I know that if I start creating one of my doozies, I'm going to have to find a thought to erase it, and I'm lazy. It has become easier to just not start cranking up the drama in the first place.

BODY TALK

Once the airways are clear and there is room for those cues, input can start to get through. Some input comes from reading body language. Once you get past the bigger gestures like a stare that could bore holes through you, or arms spread wide, (stare is bad, open arms is good), the subtler moves start speaking to you. If you were a dog, you would be noticing shifts in ear positions, stiffening of tails, changing angles of heads. As a human, small body shifts also count. With open airways, I find these subtle movements much easier to notice.

We absorb lots of body language cues as children, so we have already compiled a sizable body language dictionary for ourselves. For example, an upturned hand usually means come closer (or give it back if you are harboring stolen goods.) A raised eyebrow means disapproval. But if there's a smile attached, it's no big deal. Subtle, complex, our body language.

Once again, the steps. Open airways. Notice body language. Consult BLD (Body Language Dictionary, of course).

JUST ASK

This next cue source is so obvious it might seem ridiculous to mention. Ask for feedback. Be verbal! Ask things like, "How does this seem to you?" "What are your thoughts about____?" "Is this alright with you?"

Keeping your airways clear is critical to staying on the feedback track. If your airways aren't clear, you might have statements running through your head about wanting to be agreed with, approved of. Then when you ask for feedback, things could go very badly for you. You could find yourself knee deep in some very unpleasant stuff. You could hear yourself saying things like, "What do you *mean* you don't like this plan—I spent *hours* on it and it's just what you asked for!!!" Big communication breakdown, right? You just got sucked into the trap of mistaking feedback (a mixed bag of "this I like, this I don't like") for that seal of approval your jammed airways were clamoring for and didn't get. Just remember to keep your airways clear. Then you are free to hear the pluses *and* the minuses without a bruised ego getting in the way.

GETTING THE V'S

Another cue source is a version of unspoken messages, "getting vibes." Like the Beach Boys, "Good, good, good—good vibrations." Or, "I don't like the vibes I'm getting off you, man!" (I think that one came from a cheesy movie. Or my distant past.) Anyway, vibes are still relatively big. What they are based on is reading a sort of electrical field we each put out. Remember hearing somebody say that a room "crackled with electricity?" That would be otherwise known as vibes. They are subtle most of the time, but see if you don't start noticing them with your newly-cleared airways.

I would love to tell you that there's some kind of meter available to translate vibes, but I don't know of any. Mood rings don't work to indicate them by the way—mood rings change color with your body temperature. (A thermometer works just as well but is certainly not as attractive.) There's room for experimenting here. Try picking up vibes from people and take a stab at what they mean.

You might ask for a little feedback from them. A simple statement like "You seem ____ today" should get the ball rolling. Doing this for a while will give you a better idea of how to interpret what you are picking up, but nothing is 100 percent accurate. This is just one more way of getting cues. If it works for you, great. If it doesn't, there are other ways to get information.

WAIT FOR HUNCHES

At the far end of the input spectrum are hunches, instinct, your inner voice, intuition. They all come down to information that seems to come from the air, but feels right somehow.

It takes trust to hear information that comes in this way and actually act on it. For me, knowing that I am keeping my airways static free makes it easier to accept this kind of information. I have more confidence that the thought that just popped up is more than wishful thinking. And I have to say that I encourage stuff to drop in. Here's how I do it:

When I'm wanting information to come in this way, I will clear a larger airway space by putting my attention on getting quiet, take a moment to touch in on the area I am concerned about, and then wait. If I have the time, I will "sit with it" for as long as it feels comfortable. Sometimes nothing at all comes in. Sometimes I get a sense that I will know what to do later. Every now and again, an idea will float through. If it does, I sort of cradle it in my awareness to see how it fits. It has happened that I have gotten a sensation of something just clicking during this cradling thing. Then I feel pretty comfortable acting on the idea.

THE MATCHING GAME

Might I suggest that you play with this inner voice idea? Start with issues that aren't going to change the course of your life, like taking a moment and "checking in" on which food would be the most nourishing for you before you have a meal. First get quiet, then let your food choice come in and "sit with it" for a moment. See how it feels.

Now at the same time, using your imagination as a sensing tool, tune into what your own inner hum is like. If the food choice is not feeling like it matches with your energy, drop it and try another one. I want to add that it can happen that a good nutrition match can get overridden with pure lust for fat and sugar. For example, whipped cream. Evil! Luscious! Maybe saving desserts until you have had more practice is a good idea.

If you liked playing the matching game with food, try moving on to things you're thinking about doing. Not like using your friend's credit card to charge tickets to Hawaii or keeping the second delivery from The Sharper Image that arrived a day after the missing one—more like what to do with your free time on the weekend. Try running through a couple of options and see which one matches the best. There is no head work going on here. Stick with your sense of what feels the best. You may have to come up with a good, logical reason for everyone else, but don't worry about finding one for yourself.

This hunch-instinct-inner voice-intuition stuff is probably a little different for everyone. The common denominator is clearing the airspace and being open for a sense, an idea, to come in.

It may be that the "use it or lose it" principle affects intuition as well. It's not to suggest that your whole life should run on impulse, which could make things pretty chaotic, but just try and act on some of those hunches, exercising your inner voice, living with a little risk. That will keep your inner lines of communication open and ready for the times you really need them.

chapter 12
Going In—Going Out

I'm remembering my grandmother and how she liked to give us books she thought "the children" should read. They would usually have a cover she had made with waxed paper. We were, after all, grimy. And Grammy expected to get her book back.

The books would start their rounds with my oldest sister, who would hand them unread to my middle sister, who would then immediately give them to me. And it was my job to get them read for all of us. They were the most boring books I have ever read. I can't remember anything about them except for the "dust jackets" and the fact that I wasn't allowed to eat while I read them. I always eat when I read. Almost every book I own has cookie crumbs in the spaces between the pages.

I do think Grammy was on to us, because she began giving odd little books as gifts directly to me. To keep. I have actually read *The Water Babies*. Very dark. So it was no surprise when my high school graduation gift from her was a book, *Seeds of Contemplation* by that amazing man, Thomas Merton. I remember being impressed with the dust jacket, textured cream-colored paper with a line drawing of a stalk of wheat. I could tell right away it was an Adult Book. I had it for years before I had a clue of what it was about. I still love it. And in her honor, it hasn't got crumbs. And now I'm finally getting around to what this chapter is about—meditation. You can chalk up my interest in this to my grandmother planting her own seed with the gift of that book and Thomas Merton saying people can get past praying with words and go right on to a total immersion experience.

Meditation has a lot to do with expanding on a set of senses that come into play when you are looking more or less inward, and then once you are "in" letting that spread to "out." Then you can follow that with what feels a lot like "up." As I said, more or less.

GOING IN

Follow Your Breath

Many forms of meditation start with breathing. Pay attention to your breath as you move air in and out. Evenly. If breathing isn't an equal amount of intake and output, you get light-headed and pass out. You will get no points for achieving an altered state for that. Anyway, "following your breath," as it is often called, gets you "in" fairly quickly. It also has the advantage of being a familiar thing to do. You may have heard this exercise referred to as "getting centered." It is very soothing, especially if you take time to follow a nice deep breath in and all the way out.

You can piggyback on this and imagine breathing in nurturing, healing energy and then breathing out any tension or stress you find stored in your body. You might add a visual, like light of various colors that you are attracted to, coming in with the "in" breath. Just a few minutes of this can have some great effects. You will probably find yourself feeling calmer, more at peace, less stressed.

I'd like to mention that you can put your attention "in" more easily if the outside world isn't drawing your focus to it. One thing that helps me shut out the outside world is closing my eyes. Choosing a place that feels safe and being in a

Meditation is exercise and it has basic steps.

comfortable position will help also. If your comfortable position of choice is lying down, you might find yourself falling asleep. It does work well for this.

I'd say to forego the music at this point. I find it to be one of those "out" things to get to later once you have a firm grip on the "in" stage.

You may be getting the idea that I am seeing meditation as exercise. Definitely! Like any form of exercise, it has basic steps. And your ability to do it develops and expands just as it would with any other exercise.

One major difference between meditation and other forms of "exercise" is its versatility. You can dance as meditation, walk as meditation, not move a muscle as meditation. You can multitrack once you've had some time doing it. You can have some wonderful meditation experiences and some that seem like total blanks.

The Finding-Your-Center Exercise

Finding your center is an essential part of getting "in." Here's an exercise for finding your center that builds on the following-your-breath exercise you just tried:

➤ Do the "following your breath" exercise, allowing your focus to go all the way in and all the way out. It will probably take a few sets of inhales and exhales for you to have a good sense of slowly and easily riding your breath in and out.

➢ Now take a deep "in" breath, fully filling your lungs, and hold it for a moment. As you are holding it, become aware of how you are holding your body.

➢ Now exhale and adjust your position so it feels more in line with what feels like your center to you. You will be imagining what your center is; imaginations can be incredibly wise. If you offer yours the opportunity to identify something called "your center," it will do it.

You may only have a vague sense of "your center" at this point, or you may feel it for a few fleeting seconds. That is just fine. The next time you do this exercise, your feeling of your center will be stronger. It will develop at its own pace. So take your time with this step. And begin to enjoy the perks that come with meditation; you now have some tools to release stress, to put yourself in a peaceful state with just a few breaths.

And there's lots more to come!!!

Remember to Keep it Fun

I notice that when meditation gets mentioned, people can get very, well, serious. But you know, it can be just a plain good time. Yes, you can be getting "deep" and turn into a meditation heavy hitter *and* enjoy yourself. I see those eyes rolling in disbelief! But didn't you enjoy following your breath? Wasn't it fun to choose a color and draw it all the way in and let it flow around inside? Did you try choosing a different color to draw in every day? Did you try choosing a couple or three colors and let them twine together or maybe mix and form new colors? Try that and see if it isn't fun.

There's been a lot written about the different energies carried by specific colors. Colors are also linked to the chakras (see Chapter 10 for a refresher on chakras). I find that the colors you choose to play with usually reflect which area you could use some "fluffing up" in. But I'm getting ahead of myself. You don't need to have a comprehension of the effects of the color spectrum to use color effectively in your meditation. Each of us has a sort of inner magnet that will attract the color that will most benefit us, so you can relax about your choice and just have fun while you are deepening your capacity to meditate and drawing in the type and amount of energy that best suits your needs. And you won't run into the problem you can have with too much carrot juice of turning orange . . .

GOING OUT

So now that we've played with going in, let's try some going out:

Do the following-your-breath exercise. Give yourself a few ins and outs so you are feeling pretty, I guess you could say, clear. Sort of still inside. Now using your imagination, look around for your center, or the feeling of your center. Sit with it for a little while. Now holding this focus very gently, let your center begin to spread outward. Follow it as it moves all the way to the edges of your body.

Stop here for a moment. Take more slow deep breaths and become as fully aware of how your core energy radiates out to the edges of your body as you can. There might be a rhythm to this sensation of your core radiating out. There may be a color that you notice with your imagination. There may be a sense of warmth or tingling. You might notice a kind of enveloping somewhere around the level of your skin. Or you may draw a big blank.

If you enjoyed this, come back to it later. If it did nothing for you, feel free to skip it. We are doing this for fun, not self-torture. I notice most people don't need any suggestions from me to come up with that.

Two more things to try. These are out-of-doors things. Wait for good weather to try these out. Doing them in the wind or the rain or snow is very exhilarating, but probably a little much the first time you try them. So I'd say wait for good weather before trying them.

Choose a place you like to go and sit for a while. It's going to be easier if your place is in nature. Not necessary, but . . . you'll see why in a minute. I'm guessing you are sitting in some lush grass or at a beach or under a tree or on a favorite rock or by a lake. Do your following-your-breath exercise with your eyes closed. Now gently find your center. When you're feeling pretty cozy, shift your awareness to your skin.

Make all of these awareness shifts as gently as you can. We are looking to sense very subtle energies. It's a lot like getting a wild animal to feel safe with you. Be slow and gentle. So after you have made that gentle awareness shift from your center to your skin, notice how the sun feels on your skin. If you're in the sun, that is. If you're in the shade, notice how the shade feels. Let this soak in so that most of your awareness is on the effect the sun or shade is having on you.

Now let that go and touch back on your center for a moment. Hold that awareness of your center and, at the same time, choose something in your environment to bring into your awareness. This could be the grass, the water, a rock (if it's a big one—save little ones for later when you've had more practice), a tree.

Once you've made your choice, close your eyes. Use your imagination to find the center of what you have chosen. Hold your awareness of your center at the same time and just observe what each is like. Now open your eyes and let this go. If you enjoyed this, try it again with something else near you. This can be pretty interesting to try with asphalt, traffic lights, buildings. Explore, enjoy. You are building some very subtle sensing abilities. The more experiences you have with them, the stronger they will become.

Are you ready for the wind and the rain? Are you thinking of taking on snow? I'll walk you through the "Going Out" steps so you can give them a try.

1. Start with putting your attention on your breath. First notice how you are breathing. Now take a slow, even breath in. Hold it

for a moment and then let your breath out at the same slow, even pace. Make your "in" and "out" breaths take the same amount of time. If you don't, you'll probably hyperventilate, get dizzy, and fall down. That's not so bad in the snow. Rain is nowhere near as pleasant.

2. Advanced breathers might want to play with making a distinction between filling the upper part of your lungs (what we normally use when we're not thinking about it), and then expanding the lower part so that it feels like you are taking air into your abdomen. When you release the air, make your exhalation have two parts as well. Push the air out of the upper part of your lungs first, then the lower. It may feel like you make a little shift from upper to lower as you do this. You really get a lot of oxygen using both the upper and lower part of your lungs. Very refreshing!

3. Now let go of your focus on your breath. Gently use your imagination to find your center. Let your awareness flow into it.

4. Once you have located the feeling of your center, let your awareness radiate out from it, all the way to the edges of your body.

5. And now notice how your skin feels. Let the sensation of the air around you penetrate your skin. Notice its temperature. Notice how it moves. If you're standing out in the rain, notice the moisture in the air as it comes in contact with your skin. (If you are actually standing out in the rain, try to make it look like you are doing it on purpose, to catch a bus or something. Just standing there with a storm pouring down around you is just not, well, cool. Someone may try to lead you to safety. Or your neighbors' secret beliefs about you might move closer to being confirmed . . .)

6. Touch back on your center, going "in" again, and then go "out" and see what else you can discover. Sounds that were so far in the background that you didn't notice them may suddenly be incredibly clear. The most astounding one for me is the sound of snow falling. Notice smells. If you have been doing this with your eyes closed, open them and notice how things look.

7. Touch back on your center. Go "out" again. This time keep an awareness of your center and choose something around you

and find its center as well. Let size be no object. Hold them both, its center and yours. Now let that go. Try again, maybe changing to the other end of the scale. If you started with a tree, move to a leaf. Or move from drop of rain to a cloud. You can go to molecular if you like. I'd say start a little larger than that unless you're used to identifying things with a microscope and it's easy for you to get your awareness down to that size. Combinations are endless. Enjoy!

chapter 13
Going Up

Now you know how to go "in" and you've tried "out." Next is going up. It's probably pretty misleading to use "up" as a way to describe what I'm suggesting. "Out there" might say it. I say "up" because it has an element of inner lifting for me, and it seems to be a higher form of awareness, consciousness, whatever. "Up" might be used to describe this because we say things like "uplifted" and "that really gave me a lift" when we feel taken out of our ordinary selves and taken into our extraordinary selves. Like in that sweet old hymn, "Love Lifted Me."

The first step in "up" is shifting from sensing your physical energy to sensing yourself one step beyond that. You will still be "in there," but not as, well, physically. If this sounds confusing to you, you are on the right track. New territory! Usually starts with confusion, I find.

Begin with the usual in and out breaths; find your center; expand out from your center. Be slow and gentle and fully conscious as you do each of these steps. As you expand out from your center, notice how far out your energy envelope extends.

Notice what you do to be aware of your energy envelope. Do you perceive it containing colors? Do you notice any shapes in there? Do you "feel" it, but not "see" it? (Of course you are using your imagination as a sensing tool to do this—you've got your eyes closed and can't physically see any-thing but the insides of your eyelids, which are very dark.) Your energy envelope will probably extend outside of your physical body. See if you can get a sense of how far out it goes.

Great! Now stop and come back into your center.

When you are ready, open your eyes and come all the way back into the room.

Fun, huh? Play with this for a week or so. Make the sessions last only as long as you can do this with ease. If you find yourself pushing, it's time to stop. It isn't the length of time that makes the dif-ference with this, it's your level of awareness. If you can get a sense of your energy envelope for just a few seconds, you have been successful. Keep in mind that since the "eyes" you are using are inner eyes, they aren't limited to your physical eyes' peripheral vision—they can see a full 360 degrees. This makes it possible to see the entire envelope, front and back.

CHAKRAS

We're going to take a closer look at what might be going on in your energy envelope. I'm talking energy centers here. Those chakras, as they have been called. (You might want to refer back to Chapter 10 for a refresher on chakras.) Only we're going to do this in a sort of nonphysical way, using your inner eyes to locate them. This could take a number of sessions, so if you like to know every-thing at once, get ready to be patient. Fast is not necessarily better with this kind of stuff. Your experience of these centers is the key thing. If you can, let go of the idea of "getting it right."

The first, or root chakra, is at the base of your spine, more or less, and forms the first of a string of energy centers running vertically from here to the top of your head. There are seven basic centers in the string. You can find plenty of books writ-ten about them with theories of how they work. This means that you may want to do a little research of your own if you find yourself drawn in that direction. We're aiming here at a chance to experience them and play with how you encounter them. So for now, we're keeping it simple.

Energy center number two (which you can call the second chakra in circles where chakras are bandied about without embarrassing yourself) is half-way between the base of your spine and your belly button (okay, navel). Not surprisingly, it is seen as the creative energy center, since it lines up with reproductive organs for some of us.

The third chakra is just above your belly button. That would be your solar plexus. We could consider it your ego center.

The fourth chakra is located at the level of your heart. It is often referred to as your heart center. And the number "four" nicely lines up with a heart with four chambers. Are you noticing some relationship between these centers and how your anatomy is arranged? The alignment isn't perfect, but there is definitely a relationship. You might want to keep that in mind as you play with each center.

Number five is located over your larynx. That would be your Adam's Apple and easily noticeable if you are a guy. It is associated with self-expression, "speaking your truth." Feel free to refer to it as your throat chakra.

The sixth chakra is on your forehead. If you were to start with a point in the center of each of your eyebrows and draw lines to the center of your forehead, you would find your sixth chakra at the point of the angle these two lines form when they cross. You can use your fingers as the lines to help zero in on it. Just line up each index finger over the middle of your eyebrows, point them toward the center of your forehead, and you've got it. This center is seen as the seat of intuition and insight. You may have heard of the sixth chakra being called your third eye.

The seventh chakra is on the top of your head at the crown. As you may have guessed, it gets called your crown chakra. It is considered your link with the spiritual. That's all seven. Now let's play with them.

Exercise: Locating the Chakras
In this first exercise, the focus is on getting familiar with the location of each chakra and beginning to get a sense of its energy signature. We're going to take them one at a time, starting with the first chakra.

1. Begin by setting up your connection with your center, using the following-your-breath exercise, taking your focus to your

center, and letting your center expand out.
Take a few minutes to get settled in.

2. Now gently turn your attention to the area
   of the first or root chakra. I want to
   emphasize that this is *your* root chakra.
   Give yourself the okay to locate it where
   you imagine it to be. Use my explanation
   as a guide, but not as the absolute, defini-
   tive location. See if you can sense it in the
   general area of the base of your spine.

3. Let your awareness settle into this center.
   Now just see what you see with the eyes of
   your imagination. You may have more of a
   feeling experience than a visual experience.
   If this is your first time at playing with
   finding your chakras, the sense of them
   may be fleeting. Keep in mind that you are
   developing a new set of sensing tools. They
   need time to develop, just like any other
   skill you take on. Once you have located
   your first chakra and gotten a taste of how
   it feels, bring your focus back to your center
   and gently come back to the room.

Next time, choose the second chakra. You might
want to start by touching in on the first chakra
and then moving up to the second. Again, spend a

little time getting a sense of this center. Try out a color for it. Try a few colors and see which seem to fit the best.

Continue doing this exercise, focusing on the next chakra up the line. I would suggest focusing on one chakra in each session. Once you have done all of them, go back and play with the centers you feel drawn to. You might notice that your experience of your centers changes. Make your sessions long enough to have a sense of play but not so long that you find yourself having to push. Be light with this. Let discovery be the key element.

MAKING A LIGHT FOUNTAIN

Want to make a light fountain? We'll do this one just for fun. Do the centering process and then focus on your root chakra. Imagine it opening and drawing in a channel of energy. Imagine the energy you are drawing in to have a color that especially pleases you. Let that energy column flow up through your chakras and out the top of your head, flowing down and around your energy envelope in a continuous fountain. Change colors or add colors to the one you started with. When you have yourself good and soaked, call it a day and come gently back, letting the sensations of the colors and the chakras slowly fade. Umm-umm good!

THE CHAKRA ELEVATOR

How about combining playing with chakras and problem solving? It goes like this. Do your usual set-up, and at the end of it, run through your chakras, bottom to top. When you feel like you're pretty connected with the whole set, put your focus on the area that you want to work on. Let it assume an energy form with a shape and a color—time to use imagination as a sensing tool again—and bring it to the location of your first chakra.

See what happens. If you get nothing, move it up to the second chakra. (People who have experience with clicking and dragging their mouse may have a distinct advantage with this.) If you get some kind of feedback, like a feeling that there is any kind of interplay between the chakra energy and the energy of the issue you have chosen, or maybe a change in the way the issue looks or feels to you, just sit with it at that chakra. If you don't notice anything happening, keep moving it up. You can run through the whole string of chakras this way if it feels right for you. Stay in an observer role as much as you can. If some ideas suddenly drop in, take note of them, but let things keep

Building new ways of perceiving is like building muscle tone. It takes time.

going on their own. The idea here is that you are working apples-to-apples. So you want to stay with the energy-type of interplay and not go too much in the direction of thinking things out, which would be like bringing oranges into the apple picture. You can do that later after you finish riding this chakra elevator.

After doing this exercise, you will usually find that you either feel better about your issue and can deal with it more easily, or that you actually have some ideas about what might help.

Try it and see what it does for you. If the whole thing seems nuts to you and you draw a big blank, that's okay too. Not everything works well for everyone. And feel free to come up with your own version. They are your chakras, after all.

HOLDING TWO THINGS AS ENERGY

Now that you have some experience in orienting yourself in your energy envelope, chakras and all, you can play with holding your awareness of your self at this level while you hold something outside of yourself at the same time. Once again, keep in mind that you are exercising a new set of senses. They need to have a chance to build just like muscles.

This is the rest of the "up" part of going up. What you might want to choose to hold as something outside of yourself could be peace in its energy expression. Love, wisdom, your experience of the divine, (all of these are possibilities as well. Remember to keep this holding of your self as energy and what you choose outside of yourself an apples-to-apples event, just like with the issue you brought up your chakra elevator. So if you have chosen to experience your energy envelope as a feeling, you will be picking up on how peace (or what have you) *feels*. If you have used your inner sense of colors of light to sense your energy envelope, then find peace, etc. as *colors of light*. If you like, you can allow what you are holding to flow into your energy envelope. For example, you can have your experience of the energy of peace flow into your energy envelope and infuse and intertwine with your energy. As feeling, as color, as sound.

I want to say this can be a very powerful experience. Try not to overdo it. Let intuition guide you, remembering that more is not better. Just enough is better.

Another way to experience "going up" is to get good and settled in your energy envelope (including chakras, of course), and then go back to experience some of the things you may have tried when we were doing "going out." Rivers, rocks, trees, meadows. (You can tell I like nature.) This time, though, you will be tuning into them at this energy level. Apples-to-apples. Music, by the way, is incredible experienced from here.

It's tricky to describe these processes with words. My best advice to you is to try them and see what happens. Where you take this is pretty unlimited. It's like me telling you how to enjoy chocolate. When you know and I know that chocolate is an individual thing. I'm just hoping to make your experience of it richer and fuller for you.

chapter 14
Angels, Angels, Everywhere!

*L*et's admit it, our culture is having a giant love affair with angels. What once only showed up in some really soupy artwork, or with tiny wings and a definite tummy on Valentine's Day, is now everywhere. Recently I was given one pressed into a coin so I can tuck it discreetly into my pocket. And I won't even mention the Angel Pin Plague that swept the nation a few years back.

So what gives? Are angels just the product of wishful thinking, or have those angels been here for us all along and we're just catching on to how handy they can be?

And who are they? I say that some of them come in the form of people we know well. If you want to be able to pick them out, it's just a matter of doing what is done by artists when they want to see the design behind the shapes; they squint until their focus blurs. In this kind of soft focus, the overall design is easier to see.

Try viewing your daily encounters with that kind of soft focus, and angels may start appearing. Squinting at everyone is not the idea, though. People will just begin to think you are extraordinarily cranky and give you a wider berth. What I mean is, instead of looking at the harder edges of completing the projects, working with the stats, doing the reports, following the schedule, going to the meetings, look at the softer undercurrent. The moments when that stuff called human kindness (although I have noticed that animals have their kindnesses as well) comes bubbling up to lighten a load, or share something outrageous or fun or beautiful. This is angels at work.

Angels show up in other ways as well, more along the lines of what we have traditionally come to expect. Sometimes even reported in traditional angelic form.

Maybe the key to having angels around lies in making room for them. I'm going out on a limb and saying we should *let angels in*—and we should

Make room
for angels.

let them arrive in as many flavors as there are people. So we can have lusciously romantic ones with huge, soft wings to wrap around us and keep us safe. And we can have roguishly witty ones that like to toss in a little tease with the help they give. Or heroic ones that don't mind breaking a fall. Or angels of inspiration. Or angels of guidance.

I say this because I hold the belief that if you ask for help, you get it. And you get it in a package that is deliverable and usable. So if you can accept help in the form of an angel, an angel is what you get.

Angels seem to go for this, and I say if they're so agreeable, we should take them up on their offers.

So come on out here on this limb with me and ask for an angel. And while you're at it, ask to be introduced. Get a little communication going. We'll do it together.

ASKING FOR AN ANGEL

Be ready for some extraordinary things to begin happening. They will probably be highly personalized. I have been brought wide awake by the sound of an alarm clock when I dozed off behind the wheel on the freeway late at night. This has happened more than once. More subtle things happen so often that I'm not surprised by them any more. Things get suddenly found that I have lost, timing of events has become uncanny.

Fill out the following angel questionnaire. I mean this literally. Take out your notebook and answer these questions.

1. What kind of angel would you prefer? Angels can often have a sense of humor. Is that alright with you, or do you want a more down-to-business kind of angel? An angel that respects your choices, but isn't above reminding you what happened the last time you tried that? An angel that cheers you on?

2. How would you like your angel to communicate with you? With an image dropped into your thoughts? With words dropped into your thoughts? With maybe a sense of the chills? With sounds? These last two can be tricky to pull off. Don't be surprised if they happen only occasionally. Although I know someone with an angel called Rose who will every now and again cause a room to be filled with the fragrance of roses . . .

3. Do you want your angel to have a name? Do you want to have a visual image of

your angel? Do you want the big wings? Do you prefer more of a Light Being look? Would you rather just have a sense of the presence of your angel?

4. Do you want your angel to focus on helping in a specific area, or do you want more general overall help?

Prepare for the meeting! Now that you have done your homework and have an idea of the kind of angel you would like, make room for your angel. Hold on—I'm flashing back on Tinkerbell and Peter Pan here! No, wait! Tinkerbell is a fairy! We can skip that chant that Mary Martin did. Unless, of course, you enjoy a chant or two. If you do, be creative and make one up for your angel. Otherwise, get quiet and centered.

Using your usual meditation place is a good idea. Once you are there, open to the presence of your angel. Let your awareness of your angel's presence be whatever it might be. It could end up being entirely different from what you expected. The first time you do this, it could be quite subtle. It could also be very powerful. Just enjoy whatever happens.

Once you've had that first meeting, make a little more room for contact. So that if you could use some help during the day, an angel thought (or act) could come in. A simple reminder to yourself at the beginning of your day that you are making room for your angel should do it.

And don't forget your manners—say thank you if you suspect angel influence in something. Thank-yous count double, you know. They help you take note of when help arrives and make you more ready to accept it the next time around *and* they put the word out that you are really open to being helped. Try a thank-you when you think one is due and you'll see what I mean.

If you are enjoying this, go for more! It's entirely possible to have more than one angel. Repeat the meeting-an-angel process and see what develops.

And remember, have a good time with all of this. Regardless of what you may have been told in school, you can gain a lot more from a sense of play in what you do than you can get from making everything seem like work. And if I may be so bold as to speak for angels, they love play. But don't take my word for it, ask your angel.

What's Next

That's it! **The end of the book**, but of course not the end of what you can do with it. If you liked what you found in *Full Tilt Living*, let some of it work its way into your life. Tell friends and family what you are doing. See if they're interested in trying it with you.

Give me some feedback. Tell me what you liked and what you thought was too nuts to even consider trying. Try out the exercises and then send me an e-mail at maureensmith@fulltiltliving.com. Let me know what you think of the exercises and what happened for you. I would be delighted to post your discoveries on my Website: http://www.fulltiltliving.com.

Most of all, enjoy living *full tilt!*